# The **ESSENTIALS**® of

# **C++**

## David Hunter, Ph.D.

Professor of Computer Science
Mary Washington College
Fredericksburg, VA

*Research & Education Association*
61 Ethel Road West
Piscataway, New Jersey 08854

# THE ESSENTIALS®
# OF C++

## Year 2004 Printing

Printed in the United States of America

Library of Congress Control Number 00-132039

International Standard Book Number 0-87891-748-9

# WHAT "THE ESSENTIALS" WILL DO FOR YOU

This book is a review and study guide. It is comprehensive and it is concise.

It helps in preparing for exams and in doing homework, and remains a handy reference source at all times.

It condenses the vast amount of detail characteristic of the subject matter and summarizes the **essentials** of the field.

It will thus save hours of study and preparation time.

The book provides quick access to the important facts, principles, statements, and programming styles in the field.

Materials needed for exams can be reviewed in summary form – eliminating the need to read and re-read many pages of textbook and class notes. The summaries will even tend to bring detail to mind that had been previously read or noted.

This "ESSENTIALS" book has been prepared by an expert in the field, and has been carefully reviewed to ensure accuracy and maximum usefulness.

Dr. Max Fogiel
Program Director

# Contents

**Chapter 1**
**LANGUAGE FUNDAMENTALS**

1.1 Language Overview ........................................................... 1
1.2 Primitive Types .................................................................. 3
1.3 Constants .......................................................................... 4
1.4 Declarations ...................................................................... 5
1.5 Operators and Expressions .............................................. 5
1.6 Type Conversion ............................................................... 7
1.7 Standard Input and Output ............................................... 8

**Chapter 2**
**CONTROL STRUCTURES**

2.1 Selectional Structures ...................................................... 9
    2.1.1 The `if` Statement ............................................... 9
    2.1.2 Conditional Assignment ...................................... 11
    2.1.3 The `switch` Statement ...................................... 11
2.2 Looping Constructs .......................................................... 12
    2.2.1 The `while` Statement ........................................ 12
    2.2.2 The `for` Statement ............................................ 12
    2.2.3 The `break` and `continue` Statements .......... 13

**Chapter 3**
**NON-PRIMITIVE DATA TYPES**

3.1 Enumerated Types ............................................................ 14
3.2 Arrays ................................................................................ 15
3.3 Structures .......................................................................... 15
3.4 Unions ............................................................................... 16
3.5 The `typedef` Statement .................................................. 17

# Chapter 4
## POINTER AND REFERENCE TYPES

4.1    Pointer Variables ............................... 18

4.2    Dynamic Arrays ............................ 20

4.3    Reference Variables ..................... 20

4.4    Recursive Structures .................... 21

# Chapter 5
## FUNCTIONS

5.1    Function Structure .......................... 22

5.2    Parameter Passing Mechanisms ..................... 23

5.3    Function Return Types ..................... 24

5.4    Function Prototypes ......................... 26

5.5    Optional Parameters ...................... 26

5.6    Overloaded Functions ..................... 27

5.7    Operator Overloading ..................... 28

5.8    `inline` Functions ..................... 29

5.9    Controlling Scope and Lifetime ................ 30

       5.9.1   Scope ................. 30

       5.9.2   Lifetime .............. 30

# Chapter 6
## PREPROCESSOR DIRECTIVES AND HEADER FILES

6.1    The Preprocessor ............................ 32

6.2    Header Files and the `#include` Directive ................ 32

6.3    Symbolic Constants ......................... 33

6.4    Macros ................................ 34

6.5    Conditional Compilation ................... 34

6.6    Avoiding Duplicate Definitions ................ 35

6.7    Some Useful Library Files ................ 37

| | | |
|---|---|---|
| 6.7.1 | CTYPE.H | 37 |
| 6.7.2 | ASSERT.H | 38 |
| 6.7.3 | MATH.H | 39 |
| 6.7.4 | STDLIB.H | 40 |
| 6.7.5 | TIME.H | 41 |

## Chapter 7
## WORKING WITH CHARACTER STRINGS

| | | |
|---|---|---|
| 7.1 | Character Strings | 43 |

## Chapter 8
## CLASSES AND OBJECTS

| | | |
|---|---|---|
| 8.1 | Class Definition | 46 |
| 8.2 | The public, private, and protected Keywords | 48 |
| 8.3 | Specialized Methods | 49 |
| | 8.3.1 Constructor Methods | 49 |
| | 8.3.2 Destructor Methods | 50 |
| | 8.3.3 Copy Methods | 50 |
| | 8.3.4 Operator Methods | 51 |
| 8.4 | friend Functions | 53 |
| 8.5 | A Linked List Class | 53 |
| 8.6 | Class Nesting | 58 |
| 8.7 | static Members | 60 |
| 8.8 | Type Conversion Methods | 61 |

## Chapter 9
## INHERITANCE

| | | |
|---|---|---|
| 9.1 | Simple Inheritance | 64 |
| 9.2 | Construction and Destruction of Derived Class Objects | 65 |

9.3    Inheritance and Information Hiding ............................. 66

9.4    Multiple Inheritance ....................................... 67

9.5    `virtual` Methods and Polymorphism........................ 69

9.6    Abstract Classes ........................................... 70

## Chapter 10
## TEMPLATES

10.1   Class Templates ............................................. 72

10.2   Function Templates ......................................... 75

10.3   Templates for Derived Classes ..................................... 76

10.4   Templates for Recursive Classes ................................. 77

## Chapter 11
## INPUT AND OUTPUT

11.1   Files and Streams ............................................. 80

11.2   Overloading the Stream Operators ............................. 83

11.3   Setting Format Options ..................................... 84

11.4   Formatting and Using I/O Manipulators ....................... 86

11.5   File Classes ........................................... 87

11.6   Binary I/O ................................................. 89

## Chapter 12
## MISCELLANEOUS C++ TOPICS

12.1   Command Line Arguments ............................. 91

12.2   Functions with a Variable Number of Arguments ......... 92

12.3   Function Pointers ............................................. 95

12.4   Exception Handling........................................ 97

12.5   String Streams ............................................. 100

12.6   The `void*` Type ........................................... 100

# A word about the typographic conventions used in this book

The following typefaces have been chosen to help the reader more easily grasp and follow the concepts in this book:

C++ source code, "pseudo" code, and all program input and output are displayed in `courier`.

Special terms are displayed in *italics*.

File names are displayed in SMALL CAPS.

# CHAPTER 1

# Language Fundamentals

## 1.1 Language Overview

C++ is a superset of the C language incorporating the features of object-oriented programming. This book assumes no prior knowledge of C. In an effort to keep the text as tightly focused as possible, no attempt has been made to clarify the points at which the two languages diverge. In order to familiarize the reader with the structure of the language, an annotated C++ program is presented in Table 1.1.

The language provides two ways of specifying comments. Groups of lines may be marked as comments by bracketing them with the symbols '/*' and '*/'. Alternately, the symbol '//' marks the beginning of a comment restricted to a single line. This is the preferred method.

A C++ program need not conform to a rigid outline. Variable declarations, type definitions, and function definitions may appear in any order, provided that identifiers are declared before they are referenced. Typically, however, a C++ source file begins with a number of preprocessor directives (explained in subsequent chapters). Global type and variable definitions typically come next, followed by any number of function definitions. A C++ executable source file must contain a function called `main()`. Execution, or the start of the program, begins with this function.

Identifiers in C++ may be of any length, must start with a letter, and can contain any combination of letters, digits, and the '_' character. It uses the semi-colon as a statement separator and braces "{ }" to group statements.

**TABLE 1.1**

**An Annotated C++ Program**

```
//compiler directives always begin with #
//and are typically placed at the top of a
//file

//include the I/O functions
#include <iostream.h>

//define a constant
#define PI 3.1415927

//A function that, given a radius, returns
//the circumference of a circle
float circum(float radius)
{
   return 2*PI*radius;
}

//The main() function
void main()
{
   float r;                       //local variables
   char c = 'y';
   while (c =='y')
   {
//output newline, prompt, and read r
      cout << "\nEnter the radius of the circle: ";
      cin >> r;
//output result, and prompt to continue
      cout << "The circumference is: "
           << circum(r) << '\n';
      cout << "Enter y to continue, n to exit: ";
      cin >> c;
   }
}
```

C++ is case sensitive. Thus, the strings "SUM," "Sum," and "sum" all represent distinct identifiers. The reserved words of the language must be given in lower case and may not be used as identifiers. A complete set of reserved words is presented in Table 1.2.

**TABLE 1.2**
**C++ Reserved Words**

| | | | |
|---|---|---|---|
| sum | auto | break | case |
| catch | char | class | const |
| continue | default | delete | do |
| double | else | enum | extern |
| float | for | friend | goto |
| if | inline | int | long |
| new | operator | private | protected |
| public | register | return | short |
| signed | sizeof | static | struct |
| switch | template | this | throw |
| try | typedef | union | unsigned |
| virtual | void | volatile | while |

# 1.2  Primitive Types

The simple types provided by C++ are `int` for integers, `float` or `double` for real numbers, and `char` for characters. The distinction between `float` and `double` is machine dependent, but generally the `double` type occupies more storage and allows for greater accuracy of representation than does `float`.

Other primitive types can be produced by prefacing the simple types with the keywords `short`, `long`, `signed`, and `unsigned`. This produces types such as `long unsigned int`, `signed char`, and so forth. `signed` types can store both positive and negative numbers while `unsigned` types store only non-negative values. Consequently, `unsigned` types can store a larger range of non-negative integers than `signed` types. All integer and real types are `signed` by default, while character types are by default `unsigned`.

The meanings of the `short` and `long` modifiers are implementation dependent. Generally, however, `long` types occupy more storage than `short` types but can store a larger range of values.

It is possible to omit the `int` from a type description. Thus, the type indication `long` is equivalent to `long int`, and the indication `unsigned` is equivalent to `unsigned int`.

# 1.3 Constants

Integer constants are expressed in the usual manner: 0, 1234, -98, etc. A constant beginning with "0x" is an integer expressed in hex notation: 0x0, 0xfab5, 0x056a, etc.

Real number constants begin with a digit and contain a decimal point followed by digits. They are of type `double` by default. Constants of type `float` may be specified by affixing an 'f', as in "3.141592f".

Character constants are specified using single quotes. Non-printable characters are expressed using backslash sequences. These are presented in Table 1.3. Despite their appearance, these *escape sequences* are treated as single characters.

**TABLE 1.3**
**Special Character Constants**

| Expression | Meaning |
|:----------:|:-------:|
| \0 | ascii null (00 hex) |
| \n | newline |
| \t | horizontal tab |
| \v | vertical tab |
| \b | backspace |
| \r | carriage return |
| \f | form feed |
| \? | question mark |
| \a | audible bell |
| \\ | backslash |
| \" | double quote |
| \' | single quote |
| \ooo | octal character code |
| \xhh | hex character code |

The '\ooo' sequence allows characters to be specified as a one-, two-, or three-digit octal number. There is no limit to the number of hex digits that may be specified using the '\x' sequence. In either case, a sequence of hex or octal digits is considered to terminate at the first character that is not a legitimate digit of the specified base.

Character strings are specified using double quotes. Non-printable characters can be embedded in strings as shown in the following examples.

```
"Attention!\a\a Attention!"
"Hello World\n"
"\fPage #"
```

The use of character strings in C++ programming is fully explored in a subsequent chapter.

## 1.4   Declarations

Variable declarations in C++ consist of a type name followed by one or more variable names. Optionally, declarations may specify default values for variables. Below are some examples of C++ variable declarations:

```
long int i, j, k;
int sum = 0, count = 0;
char c = '\0';
```

Any declaration can be preceded by the keyword `const`. This marks the identifier as being a read-only value. That is, its value may be accessed but not modified.

```
const float pi = 3.1415927;
```

## 1.5   Operators and Expressions

Table 1.4 presents the most commonly used C++ operators. Many of these are explained in subsequent chapters. The operators are grouped according to precedence, from highest precedence to lowest precedence. Unary and assignment operators are right associative, while all others are left associative.

The logical operators result in a value of zero for false and one for true. Evaluation of logical expressions stops as soon as the result of the expression can be determined. For example, given the expression `(expr1) && (expr2) && (expr3)`, if `expr1` is false, then `expr2` and `expr3` are not evaluated. Since `expr1` is false the entire expression will be false regardless of the values of `expr2` and `expr3`. Similarly, if `expr1` was true and `expr2` was false, `expr3` would not be evaluated. Expressions involving logical OR are evaluated until a true expression is encountered.

Two of the more specialized operators in C++ are the `increment` '++' and `decrement` '--' operators. These operators, quite simply, increment or decrement a variable by one. Thus, the expression `++i` is equivalent to the assignment statement `i = i + 1`, and `--i` is equivalent to `i = i - 1`.

**TABLE 1.4**

| | |
|---|---|
| ++, --, !, ~ | Increment, decrement, logical not, bitwise not |
| (type) | Type cast |
| *, /, % | Multiplication, division, remainder |
| +, - | Addition, subtraction |
| <<, >> | Bit shift left, Bit shift right |
| <, <=, >, >= | Relational operators |
| ==, != | Equals, not equals |
| & | Bitwise and |
| ^ | Bitwise xor |
| \| | Bitwise or |
| && | Logical and |
| \|\| | Logical or |
| =, +=, -=, *=, /= | Assignment |

Furthermore, these operators have different semantics depending upon whether they appear to the left or right of a variable. The distinction is illustrated here:

```
i = 10;
j = ++i + 5; //j is 16 and i is 11
i = 10;
j = i++ + 5; //j is 15 and i is 11
```

In the first sequence, because the increment operator appears to the left of `i` it performs a pre-increment. In the second example it appears to the right and therefore performs a post-increment. That is, in the first example `i` is incremented before the addition; in the second it is incremented after the addition.

Assignment in C++ is treated no differently than other operators. It may therefore appear anywhere within an expression, as illustrated below.

```
float x, y;
int i = 10, j = 3;
```

```
y = (x = i) / j; //x is now 10, y is 3.333
float x, y;
int i = 10, j = 3;
y = x = i / j; //x and y are both 3
```

Also, because the operator is right associative, assignment statements with multiple targets such as x = y = z = 10.0 are acceptable.

In addition to the '=' assignment operator, C++ also defines a set of operators that combine arithmetic and assignment. For example, the statement i *= j is equivalent to i = i * j. In general, the expression i op= j is equivalent to i = i op j where op is an arithmetic, or bitwise, operator.

# 1.6   Type Conversion

C++ does a great deal of automatic type conversion in expressions and assignment statements. When expressions involve a mixture of long and short (or float and double) variables C++ will convert all operands to the longer type and perform the specified operation. When expressions include both integers and reals, C++ converts the integers to reals and performs the operation. When the division operator is used on two integers, the quotient is truncated and the result is an integer. This can cause some unintended results, as illustrated by the sequence below.

```
float x;
int i = 10, j = 3;
x = i / j;
```

Because i and j are both integers, integer division is performed and x is assigned the value 3, not 3.33333 as one might expect.

Character values may also be intermixed with reals and integers. In these cases, the integer value of the character is its ASCII value.

Shorter values may be assigned to longer variables with no side effects. long values may also be assigned to short variables, but doing so may result in a corrupted value since the high order bits of the long value are lost. Real values are truncated when assigned to integer variables. The effect of assigning `double` values to `float` variables is machine dependent. Usually, they will be rounded or truncated.

Type conversion can be made explicit through the use of a *type cast*. A type cast has the form `(type) expression` and indicates that the expression is to be converted into the specified type. Type casting can be used to avert the problem identified earlier.

```
float x;
int i = 10, j = 3;
x = (float) i / (float) j;
```

In this example, `i` and `j` are explicitly converted to `float` type and floating-point division is therefore performed. Because implicit type conversion can have unintended side effects, it is recommended that programmers use explicit type casting whenever type conversion must occur.

## 1.7   Standard Input and Output

Unfortunately, a complete understanding of C++ I/O cannot be reached until one has first grasped the concepts of objects and software libraries. Therefore, a thorough discussion of this topic is left for a later chapter. In order to use I/O in subsequent examples, however, the syntax is introduced here.

To read a series of values from standard input into a series of variables, one uses a statement of the form:

```
cin >> var1 >> var2 >> var3;
```

Variables are assigned values in order as they are encountered on the standard input device. Whitespaces (blanks, tabs, and newlines) are skipped. The list of values read is called an *input stream*.

Similarly, to write a series of values to standard *output*, one uses a statement of the form:

```
cout << val1 << val2 << val3;
```

Note that new lines are not generated unless explicitly included in the output stream as shown below:

```
cout << "The result is: " << result << '\n';
```

To provide access to these facilities a program must contain the statement `#include <iostream.h>`, usually placed at the top of a source file.

# CHAPTER 2

# Control Structures

## 2.1  Selectional Structures

### 2.1.1  The **if** Statement

The most general form of the if statement is:

```
if (expression)
{
   statement;
   statement;
   ...
}
else
{
   statement;
   statement;
   ...
}
```

If only one statement appears in one of the branches, then the braces are not required, as illustrated here:

```
if (expression)
   statement;
else
   statement;
```

The expression to be tested must be enclosed in parentheses. The `else` portion is optional. Grouping symbols in the `if` and the `else` are not required if only one statement is to be selected.

Because C++ has no Boolean data type, any legitimate C++ expression, including assignments and I/O, may be the subject of an `if` statement. Whatever expression is specified is evaluated and, if non-zero, the "true" branch of the `if` is executed. If the expression results in a value of zero, the "false" branch is executed.

This open-ended nature of the `if` is a frequent cause of error for beginning C++ programmers, as shown in the examples below.

```
if (a = 10) //SERIOUS BUG!
{
  ...
}
if ((a > b) & (c < d)) //SERIOUS BUG!
{
  ...
}
if (!a > b) //SERIOUS BUG!
{
  ...
}
```

In the first example, the programmer has intended to test if a is equal to 10. Instead, the code assigns 10 to a then executes the body of the `if`. The `if` body will always be executed because 10 is non-zero. In the second example, a logical AND was intended but instead a bitwise AND is performed on the results of the expressions (a > b) and (c < d). Finally, in the third example, since the NOT operator has a higher precedence than the *greater than* operator, the expression first performs logical NOT on a, then compares the result to b.

## 2.1.2  Conditional Assignment

C++ allows statements of the form `if (test) var = val1 else var = val2` to be written using the notation `var = test ? val1 : val2`. For example, the statement

```
a = n > 10 ? b : c;
```

is equivalent to the statement

```
if (n > 10)
  a = b;
else
  a = c;
```

## 2.1.3  The `switch` Statement

The `switch` statement is used to select statements based on the value of a variable. In the example provided below, the first group of statements is executed if `expression` is equal to `value1`, the second group if `expression` is either `value2` or `value3`, and the third group is selected if none of the other cases apply. The `break` statement transfers control out of the `switch`.

```
switch (expression)
{
  case value1 : statement;
            statement;
            ...
            break;
  case value2 :
  case value3 : statement;
            statement;
            ...
            break;
  default : statement;
        statement;
}
```

When a `switch` statement is encountered, the specified expression is evaluated and an appropriate case selected. Execution begins at that point and continues downward until either a `break` is executed or the end of the `switch` is reached.

## 2.2 Looping Constructs

### 2.2.1 The `while` Statement

The two logic controlled loops in C++ are illustrated below.

```
while (expression)
{
  statement;
  . . .
}
do
{
statement;
. . .
} while
(expression);
```

### 2.2.2 The `for` Statement

The other looping construct in C++ is the for loop.

```
for (initial expression;
     while test;
     increment expression)
{
  statement;
  statement;
  . . .
}
```

The initial expression is evaluated once, upon entering the loop. The loop continues execution as long as the while test is true (non-zero). After each loop iteration (essentially, as the last statement of the loop body) the increment is performed. A standard count loop that iterates from 1 to 10 can therefore be implemented as:

```
for (i = 1; i <= 10; ++i)
{
```

```
do something;
}
```

Since any legitimate C++ expression may be used in any of the three posi-
tions of the `for` statement, this construct is considerably more general than
that provided by most other languages.

## 2.2.3   The **break** and **continue** Statements

The `break` statement may be used to terminate a loop at any point. It
transfers control to the first statement after the loop. The `continue` statement
causes the loop to skip to its next iteration, essentially transferring control to
the `while`, `do`, or `for` statement.

# CHAPTER 3

# Non-Primitive Data Types

## 3.1   Enumerated Types

Enumerated types are defined as illustrated below.

```
enum weekday {Monday, Tuesday, Wednesday, Thursday,
Friday};
```

The values listed within the braces are called enumeration constants and are given integer values starting at zero. Variables of type enum may therefore appear anywhere integers may appear. However, some compilers will not allow integers to be directly assigned to enumerated types. Thus, the following is a potential compilation error:

```
weekday d;
int i = 3;
d = i; //not allowed by some compilers!
```

Should one wish to do this, a type cast should be performed as illustrated below:

```
weekday d;
int i = 3;
d = (weekday) i;
```

The effect is to assign d the enumerated constant Wednesday. Since most

C++ implementations will not provide range checking unless specifically told to do so, programmers should be careful to avoid sequences such as:

```
int i = 10;

...

d = (weekday) i; //executable but bugged
```

## 3.2  Arrays

An array definition and initialization are illustrated below.

```
int a[5] = {2,3,5,7,11};
```

This declares a to be an array of five integers and initializes it to contain the first five prime numbers. Array indices in C++ are numbered starting at zero and not at one. Thus, a[0] and a[4] are acceptable references, but a[5] does not exist. Again, range checking is usually not provided by default.

The language does not support multidimensional arrays in the traditional sense. However, defining arrays of arrays has the same effect. Thus, one might define a matrix as:

```
float matrix[100][100];
```

The notation matrix[1][10] refers to the element at row 1 column 10.

Arrays cannot be copied using the assignment operator. Thus, the following code sequence is illegal.

```
int a[5], b[5];

...

a = b; //ILLEGAL!
```

## 3.3  Structures

Structures in C++ are the equivalent of what are called *records* in some other languages. They represent aggregations of related data items. Their declaration and initialization is illustrated below.

```
struct student_record {
  int id;
  char classification;
  float gpa;
```

```
};
student_record r = {1012, 'J', 3.25};
```

The dot operator '.' is used to access components of a record. Thus, one could say r.id or r.gpa, for example.

Structure variables may be used with the assignment operator. Thus, one may write:

```
student_record r = {1012, 'J', 3.25}, s;
...
s = r;
...
```

## 3.4  Unions

A union is a structure in which all fields begin at the same memory address. A union occupies sufficient memory to store its largest field. In a union a single storage location may store values of different types, as illustrated below.

```
union union_example {
 int integer_value;
 float float_value;
};
main()
{
 union_example u;
 u.integer_value = 12;
 cout << u.float_value;
}
```

Since u.integer_value and u.float_value occupy that same storage, the example stores the bit pattern for 12 in u then writes out whatever floating-point number that bit pattern represents. A reference to u.integer_value interprets the value stored at u as an integer, while a reference to u.float_value interprets the value as a float.

The union is a potentially unsafe construct but can be convenient when used as fields within a structure, as in the example shown on the next page. In this example, a union is used to declare an array of grades each of which can be either a letter grade or a numerical score.

```
union grade_value {
  float score;
  char letter;
};
enum grade_type {letter_grade, numerical_grade};
struct result_record {
  grade_type type;
  grade_value value;
};
main()
{
  result_record results[25];
  results[1].type = letter_grade;
  results[1].value = 'A';
  ...
  results[20].type = numerical_grade;
  results[20].value = 85;
  ...
}
```

## 3.5 The typedef Statement

The typedef statement is used to create new type identifiers, as illustrated below.

```
typedef float Temperature;
typedef char String32[32];
typedef float Matrix[100][100];
```

The typedef statement consists of the reserved word typedef followed by an ordinary declaration statement. Subsequent to the sample statements, the declaration Temperature t would be equivalent to float t, the declaration String32 s would be equivalent to char s[32], and Matrix m would be equivalent to float m[100][100].

17

# CHAPTER 4

# Pointer and Reference Types

## 4.1   Pointer Variables

A *pointer* variable is one that contains the address of a storage location. The '*' operator is used to declare that a variable is a pointer. For example, the declaration int* p means that p will be a pointer to (i.e., contain the address of) a location at which an integer is stored. Alternately, one can declare several pointers to integers with the statement int* p, *q, *r, *s. Once a pointer variable p has been assigned a value (i.e., made to point to something) the identifier *p is used to reference the location to which p points. Accessing *p is called *dereferencing* the pointer.

One way to assign a pointer variable a value (which should be an address) is to use the reference '&' operator, which returns the address of its operand. This is illustrated below.

```
int* p, i = 15;
p = &i;              //p contains the address of I
*p = 20              //put 20 in memory at address
                     //stored in p (this will be I)
cout << i;           //outputting i displays 20
```

In this example, both *p and i refer to the same storage cell. This situation, in which a storage location can be referred to by more than one identifier, is called *aliasing*.

Pointer variables can also be given values by assigning to them the results of a new operation. The new operator allocates a storage unit for a specified type and returns the address of the allocated unit. Thus, the statement p = new int allocates storage for an integer and puts its address in p. If there is insufficient storage to allocate a variable of the specified type, *new* returns a value of zero.

The reverse of new is delete. The delete operator is used to deallocate storage allocated by new. The statement delete p means "return the storage unit whose address is in p to the pool of available storage units."

Pointer variables which have not yet been made to point to something should be assigned the value 0. It is traditional to use a symbolic constant called NULL to represent this value. Thus, sequences such as the following are frequently seen:

```
#define NULL 0
...
void main()
{
  int *p = NULL, *q = NULL;
  ...
  if (p == NULL) p = new int;
  ...
}
```

Pointer variables can be made the subject of arithmetic operations. When used with pointer variables, the increment and decrement operators are indexed according to the size of the data type they point to. That is, the expression ++p is equivalent to p = p + s, where s is the size of the data type pointed to by p. Pointer arithmetic is considered archaic in C++ and is not recommended.

The '->' operator is used to reference the individual fields of a structure that are referenced by a pointer. The expression p->f is equivalent to (*p).f. The use of pointers with structures is illustrated below:

```
student_record *p;
```

```
p = new student_record;
p->id = 1013;
p->classification = 'F';
...
delete p;
```

## 4.2   Dynamic Arrays

Pointers can be used to implement arrays whose size is not known until run time. These are known as dynamically allocated arrays. The method is illustrated below.

```
int *a, size;
cout << "how many data points are there?";
cin >> size;
a = new int[size];
for (int i = 0; I < size-1; ++I)
  cin >> a[i];
delete[] a;
```

The subscript operator '[ ]' can be used to index any pointer variable. Given that p is a pointer, the expression p[n] returns the value at address p+n*s, where s is the size of the data type pointed to by p.

## 4.3   Reference Variables

Like pointers, reference variables contain the address of a memory cell. Reference variables are declared as type& var1 = var2. They must be given an initial value when declared, and the value must be something which has an address, not a constant or an expression. The effect of the declaration is to make var1 an alias for var2. The association between a reference variable and the variable it aliases cannot be changed. The example below illustrates the workings of reference variables.

```
int i = 15, j = 50;
int& p = i;  //p is an alias for i
p = 20;      //really sets i to 20
cout << i;   //print 20
```

One cannot create arrays of references, nor pointers to references.

## 4.4   Recursive Structures

A recursive data type is one which makes a reference to itself. For example, a linked list is a recursive data structure since each element of the list contains a pointer to the next element in the list. The example below illustrates how to define a linked list of character values in C++.

```
struct ListCell {
  char contents;
 ListCell *next;
 };
```

# CHAPTER 5

# Functions

## 5.1 Function Structure

A typical C++ function definition is shown below.

```
int power(int base, int exponent)
{
    int product = 1;
    for (int i = 1; i <= exponent; ++i)
    product = product * base;
    return product;
}
```

A function may contain any number of `return` statements. A function terminates with the value specified as soon as any `return` is encountered. Local variables may be declared anywhere within the function provided they are declared before they are referenced.

C++ does not make a distinction between *functions* and *procedures*. All subroutines in C++ are considered functions. However, procedures may be emulated by declaring a function to be of type `void`. Such functions need not include `return` statements. Functions for which no type is specified (not even `void`) are considered to be of type `int`.

Functions that do not have parameters may be specified using either the notation `type f()` or `type f(void)`. When functions without parameters are called, the notation `f()` must be specified.

## 5.2 Parameter Passing Mechanisms

C++ provides two fundamental mechanisms for passing parameters to functions: pass by value and pass by reference. With the exception of array parameters, which are discussed later, pass by value is the default mechanism. When this mechanism is used, the parameter values in the function call (*actual parameters*) are copied into the parameters declared in the function definition (*formal parameters*). Modifying a formal parameter passed by value has no effect on its corresponding actual parameter.

When the pass by reference method is used, a formal parameter becomes an alias for its corresponding actual parameter. Changes made to the formal parameter are immediately reflected in the actual parameter. The '&' symbol is used to indicate that a parameter should be implemented using the reference method.

The overhead involved in copying values from actual to formal parameters can make the pass by value method inappropriate for structures. Consequently, many programmers prefer to pass structures (and objects, as seen later) by reference and pass scalars (integers, reals, and so forth) by value.

Both types of parameters may be prefaced with `const` to indicate that they are read only parameters. Such parameters can have their values accessed, but cannot be assigned to.

When arrays are used as actual parameters, the corresponding formal parameter is treated as a pointer to the first element of the array. This is illustrated in the example below.

```
void read_array(int* a, int& size)
{
  cout >> "How many data points?";
  cin >> size;
  cout << "Enter data: ";
  for (int I = 0; I < size; ++I)
    cin >> a[i];
```

```
}

int sum(const int *a, const int size)
{
   int temp = 0;
   for (int I = 0; I < size; ++I)
     temp = temp + a[i];
   return temp;
}

void main()
{
   int data[100], n;
   read_array(data, n);
   cout << "Sum is:"<< sum(data,n);
}
```

One could write `int a[]` in place of `int* a` in the two function defini-tions. The effect is the same. While the former is more readable, the latter has been used to more clearly indicate the semantics of array parameter passing. The `const` qualification of the parameters in `sum()` is not necessary for cor-rectness, but since both parameters are used in a read-only manner they have been so marked.

## 5.3   Function Return Types

A function may return a value of any type including structured types, point-ers, and references. Examples of the former two types are shown below.

```
student_record read_record_method1()
//return a student record
{
 student_record r;
 cin >> r.id >> r.classification >> r.gpa;
 return r;
```

```
}
student_record *read_record_method2()
//return a pointer to a student record
{
   student_record *r;
   r = new student_record;
   cin >> r->id >> r->classification
       >> r->gpa;
   return r;
}
void main()
{
 student_record test1, *test2;
 test1 = read_record_method1();
 test2 = read_record_method2();
 cout << test1.id << test2->id;
}
```

Functions that return reference types should not be thought of as returning values but as aliases for storage locations. The function call becomes an alias for the storage location returned by the function. In the example below, the max() function returns an alias for the larger of its two parameters.

```
int& max(int& a, int& b)
{
   if (a > b)
     return a;
   else
     return b;
}

void main()
{
   int q = 5, r = 10, s = 15, t = 20;
   ++max(q,r);                //increments r
```

```
   max(s,t) = 3;               //t = 3
   int x = max(q,s)            //x = 15
}
```

## 5.4  Function Prototypes

A function prototype specifies the name of a function and the type and number of its parameters, as illustrated below.

```
int power(int, int);
```

Function prototypes allow a programmer to reference a function before its implementation is specified. They also allow sets of related function definitions to be grouped into *header* files as discussed in the next chapter.

## 5.5  Optional Parameters

C++ allows function parameters to be given default values, essentially making them optional parameters. This technique is illustrated below.

```
int volume(int width,
           int length = 2,
           int height = 1)
{
   return width*length*height;
}


void main()
{
   int test;
   test = volume(3,2,2);       //test is 12
   test = volume(3,2);         //test is 6
   test = volume(2);           //test is 4
}
```

Since no value was specified for height in the second call to volume(),
it was assigned a default value of 1, and in the third call to volume() both
height and width were assigned their default values.

Once a formal parameter is specified as having a default value, all subsequent formal parameters must also be given default values. Thus the following function is not permissible.

```
int volume(int width, int length = 2,
              int height) //NOT ALLOWED!
{
   return width*length*height;
}
```

Similarly, it is not possible to leave "holes" in either the formal or actual parameter lists. Thus, it would not be possible to call volume() specifying only width and height.

Default parameter values for a function can be specified only once. They cannot be specified in both a function's prototype and its implementation. If function prototypes are used, it is recommended that default parameters be specified there, as illustrated below.

```
//specify defaults in prototype
int volume(int, int = 2, int = 1);

//do not specify them here
int volume(int width, int length, int height)
{
   return width*length*height;
}
```

## 5.6   Overloaded Functions

It is possible in C++ to define several functions with identical names, provided that they differ in their return types or their formal parameter lists. This is illustrated below.

```
struct fraction {
  int numerator, denominator;
```

```
}

void write(int a[], int size)
{
  for (int i = 0; i <= size-1; ++i)
    cout << a[i] << '\n';
}

void write(char a[], int size)
{
  for (int i = 0; i <= size-1; ++i)
    cout << a[i] << '\n';
}

void write(fraction f)
{
  cout << f.numerator << '/'
    << f.denominator;
}
```

The compiler is able to decipher any call to `write()` by checking the types of the actual parameters.

When several definitions are associated with the same name, that name is said to be *overloaded*. Thus, the example above illustrates function overloading.

## 5.7 Operator Overloading

One may overload operators as well as functions. In the example below, the multiplication operator is "told" how to multiply two fraction structures.

```
fraction operator *(fraction f1, fraction f2)
{
  fraction result;
  result.numerator = f1.numerator*f2.numerator;
```

```
  result.denominator =
     f1.denominator*f2.denominator;
  return result;
}


void main()
{
  fraction a = (2,3), b = (3,5), c;
  c = a * b; //c is 6/15
}
```

The first parameter in a binary operator definition is the left operand and the second is the right operand.

One may only overload existing C++ operators. It is not possible to create new operator symbols, and it is not possible to change the associativity and precedence of an operator.

## 5.8  `inline` Functions

The run-time overhead associated with function calls makes it inefficient to call functions that contain only a few lines of code since the time spent in the function may be significantly less than the time required to pass the parameters, transfer control, return the value of the function, and so forth. Consequently, C++ allows programmers to specify that a function is to be implemented `inline`.

When the compiler encounters a call to a function marked as `inline`, it does not generate a function call but instead substitutes the body of the function in the place of the function call. An `inline` function definition is shown below.

```
inline int double(int x)
{
  return 2 * x;
}
```

## 5.9    Controlling Scope and Lifetime

### 5.9.1    Scope

Scope refers to the range of statements over which a variable can be referenced. Generally, the scope of a variable in C++ proceeds from the point at which it is declared to the end of the program unit (function or file) in which it is declared. Later, it will be shown that the scope of a variable defined within a class structure is more tightly restricted than this.

The scope resolution operator ': :' can be used to reference variables which would otherwise not be accessible. This is illustrated below.

```
int i; //variable is accessible from this
        //point onward


float fn()
{
  int i; //references to i within fn() refer to
         //this variable. The previously
         //declared i is now "blocked"and can
         //only be accessed by using the ::
         //operator.

  cout << i;    //write out value of local i
  cout << ::i; //write out value of
               //externally declared i.
}
```

### 5.9.2    Lifetime

The lifetime of a variable refers to the time during which storage for the variable has been allocated. Unless otherwise stated, storage for a variable is allocated when that variable is declared and deallocated when the unit in which it is declared terminates. Thus, variables declared within functions are newly created every time the function is activated and destroyed when the function terminates. This is not always desirable, however, and can be overridden in C++ by declaring a variable to be static.

Storage for a static variable is allocated the first time its declaration statement is encountered and is not deallocated until the entire C++ program terminates. For example, the function below displays 1 the first time it is called, 2 the second time, 3 the third time, and so forth. If a were not declared static, it would print 1 each time it was called.

```
void fn()
{
  static int a = 0;
  a = a + 1;
  cout << a;
}
```

# CHAPTER 6

# Preprocessor Directives and Header Files

## 6.1   The Preprocessor

Before the translation phase of compilation begins, a C++ program is first treated by the C++ preprocessor. The preprocessor performs several tasks, the most significant of which are:

1. Copy specified files into the current source file.

2. Perform text substitutions in the source file.

3. Select sections of code to be compiled or skipped by the compiler.

Instructions to the preprocessor are given through *directives*. These are indicated by the '#' symbol and must not be preceded by white space.

## 6.2   Header Files and the `#include` Directive

The `#include filename` directive is used to copy a specified file into the file being processed. If the file name is enclosed in angle brackets, the preprocessor will search for the file on the system "include file" search path. If the name is enclosed in double quotes, the preprocessor will search for the file on the user's current directory.

```
#include <iostream.h>
#include "myfile.h"
```

The #include directive is most often used to provide programmers access to groups of related type definitions and function prototypes located in *header* files. Header files are traditionally given a file extension of H to distinguish them from source code files which are usually given an extension of CC, CPP, or C. C++ installations usually provide a large set of header files defining functions for tasks such as string manipulation, I/O, mathematical computation, and so forth.

Some header files are standard and will be included with every C++ installation. For example, the file iostream.h and string.h provide I/O and string manipulation functions, respectively. These are discussed in later chapters. Some of the other standard header files are discussed at the end of this chapter, but a complete treatment is beyond the scope of this book. Programmers should consult their compiler documentation for a description of what has been included in their implementation.

Header files should contain only definitions and function prototypes. Associated with a header file will be a corresponding source code file that contains the complete specification of the functions whose prototypes appear in the header file. To create a C++ executable file, each source code file is compiled separately and the resulting object code files linked using a system linker. (Usually, the same program that provides compilation can also provide linking.)

## 6.3   Symbolic Constants

The #define directive can be used to define symbolic constants, as shown below.

```
#define PI 3.1415927
#define MAX_SIZE 100
#define ERROR "An error has occurred."
```

Symbols defined this way are quite different from those defined using the const declaration shown in Chapter 1. The former exist only during the preprocessing stage, while the latter are compiled in a way much like variables.

Symbolic constants defined this way instruct the preprocessor to perform text substitution. That is, with reference to the example above, the preprocessor will simply substitute the string "3.1415927" whenever it encounters PI in the source file. After preprocessing, the resulting altered text is made the subject of the compiler, which consequently never "sees" PI.

## 6.4 Macros

Macros are another form of text substitution that can be specified using the #define directive. A macro is defined with parameters and takes the general form:

```
#define name(arg1, arg2, ...) substitute-text
```

For example, one might define the following:

```
#define sqr(x) (x)*(x)
```

Subsequent to this definition, upon encountering the text sqr(a) the pre-processor substitutes (a)*(a), upon encountering sqr(a+b) it substitutes (a+b)*(a+b), and so forth. Since the preprocessor performs text substitution only, upon encountering sqr("Hello world") it would substitute ("Hello world")*("Hello world") and proceed with its processing.

The last example illustrates that macros are potentially very unsafe constructs. In fact, they are a holdover from C. Since they provide functionality very similar to that provided by inline functions, there is no reason to use them in C++ and they should be avoided.

## 6.5 Conditional Compilation

A programmer can cause the preprocessor to select sections of code to be compiled or not compiled by using either the #ifdef ("if defined") or #ifndef ("if not defined") directives. The two have the same form. The #ifdef is shown below.

```
#ifdef symbol
... some code ...
#else
... some code ...
#endif
```

The code contained within the "if" section of the block is compiled if the specified symbol is known to the preprocessor. If the symbol is not known, the code within the "else" section is compiled. The effect of the #ifndef directive is analogous. In either case, the #else is optional. Symbols can be defined by statements of the form #define symbol.

These directives are very useful if a program must include machine specific sections of code. The technique is illustrated below.

```
#ifdef MS_DOS
  //code specific to MS_DOS
#endif
#ifdef UNIX
  //code specific to UNIX
#endif
```

To compile this code for a specific platform, a programmer may include either the line #define MS_DOS or #define UNIX at the top of the source file. Only the appropriate blocks of code are then compiled.

## 6.6 Avoiding Duplicate Definitions

Header files and the #include directive provide a simple mechanism for creating software libraries but can cause problems since it is easily possible for the same header files to be copied several times into the same source file. The problem is illustrated below.

```
//This is the file class.h
#include "student.h"
struct class_record {
 student_record students[100];
 int enrollment;
}
...
//This is the file grade_book.cc
#include "student.h"
#include "class.h"
```

In the example, the definitions in STUDENT.H end up being copied into GRADE_BOOK.CC twice: once as a direct consequence of #include "student.h" and indirectly from #include "class.h" because CLASS.H also includes STUDENT.H. Compiler errors will be generated for every duplicate definition. Of course, a careful programmer could avoid this problem by not including STUDENT.H in GRADE_BOOK.CC, but for large systems with many different header files it is difficult or impossible to keep an accurate track of which files are included in which other files.

Because of this problem, it is common practice to associate with each header file a preprocessor symbol that serves as a flag to indicate whether or not the contents of that file have been compiled. This technique is illustrated below. In the example, the GRADE_BOOK.CC file may contain more than one copy of STUDENT.H, but the definitions are compiled only the first time they are encountered.

STUDENT.H

```
#ifndef student
#define student
struct student_record {
  int id;
  char classification;
  float gpa;
};
void read_student(student_record&);
#endif //the last statement in the file
```

CLASS.H

```
#ifndef class
#define class
#include "student.h"
struct class_record {
```

```
  student_record students[100];
  int enrollment;
}
...
#endif //the last statement in the file
```

GRADE_BOOK.CC
```
#include "student.h"
#include "class.h"
void main()
{
  student s;
  class c;
  ...
}
```

## 6.7    Some Useful Library Files

### 6.7.1    CTYPE.H

The header file CTYPE.H defines several functions for testing character data. In the table below, the specified function is true if the argument is in the specified range.

**TABLE 6.1**

| | |
|---|---|
| `int isalnum(int)` | upper or lower case letter or digit |
| `int islower(int)` | lower case letter |
| `int isalpha(int)` | upper or lower case letter |
| `int isprint(int)` | a printing character, 0x20 – 0x7E |
| `int isascii(int)` | low order byte range 0 – 127 |
| `int ispunct(int)` | a punctuation character (`isspace()` or `iscntrl()`) |
| `int iscntrl(int)` | a delete or control character, 0x7F or 0x00 – 0x1F |
| `int isspace(int)` | space, tab, carriage return, newline, vertical tab, or form feed |
| `int isdigit(int)` | a digit |
| `int isupper(int)` | an upper case letter |
| `int isgraph(int)` | like `isprint()` except the space character is excluded |
| `int isxdigit(int)` | is a hex digit, 0 – 9 and A – F |

In addition to these, the file defines functions `int toupper(int)` and `int tolower(int)`. These convert letters to upper and lower case, respectively. They return an unchanged copy of their argument if it is not a character in the expected range.

### 6.7.2 ASSERT.H

The header file ASSERT.H defines a macro called `assert`, which is used to specify truth conditions at various places in a program. These *assertions* state properties that should be true if the program is operating correctly, as in the example below.

```
//return first character in a list
char first(ListCell* List)
{
  assert(List != NULL);
  return List->contents;
}
```

If an assertion is encountered and its specified condition is evaluated as false, the program is terminated and an appropriate error message displayed. (The particular message is machine dependent, but usually it specifies the function and line where the failed assertion occurred.)

Assertions are extremely useful debugging aids but will increase the size of an object file. Therefore, the macro is designed so that `assert` statements will be compiled only if the symbol NODEBUG is not defined.

### 6.7.3 MATH.H

The file MATH.H contains functions useful for performing mathematical computations. Some of them are given below. Typically, several variations of each function are defined to operate with different data types. The functions below accept arguments of type `double`.

**TABLE 6.2**

| | |
|---|---|
| `sin(), cos(), tan()` | Trigonometric function |
| `asin(), acos(), atan()` | Arc-trigonometric functions |
| `sinh(), cosh(), tanh()` | Hyperbolic functions |
| `log(), log10()` | Natural and base-10 logarithm |
| `exp(e,x)` | e to the power of x |
| `ciel(x)` | Finds smallest integer not less than x |
| `floor(x)` | Finds largest integer not greater than x |
| `sqrt(x)` | Square root of x |
| `abs(x)` | Absolute value of x |
| `pow(base, exponent)` | Power (exponentiation) |

## 6.7.4 STDLIB.H

This file contains a miscellaneous group of definitions that are too numerous to list exhaustively. Some of the more frequently used functions are given in the table below.

**TABLE 6.3**

| | |
|---|---|
| `int atoi(char*s)` | Convert a string of characters to an integer |
| `float atof(char*s)` | Convert a string of characters to type `float` |
| `int exit(int)` | Exit the program and return the specified value |
| RAND_MAX | A symbol representing the largest random number generated by `rand()` |
| NULL | Symbol representing an "empty" pointer |
| `int rand()` | Return a pseudo-random integer in the range 0 to RAND_MAX |
| `srand(unsigned int)` | Set the seed value used by `rand()` |
| `double strtod(char*s)` | Convert character string to type `double` |
| `long strtoll(char*s)` | Convert character string to type `long` |
| `unsigned long strtoul(char*s)` | Convert character string to type `unsigned long` |

```
#include <stdio.h>
#include <stdlib.h>
#include <time.h>

void main ()
{
 int head=0, tails =0;
 time_t t = time (NULL);
 srand (t);
 for (int i=1; i <= 100; ++i)
      if (rand() % 2 == 0)
        ++heads;
```

40

```
    else
      ++tails;
    cout << heads << tails;
}
```

A program illustrating the use of the random number generator is given above. The program simulates the toss of 100 coins. The srand() function should be called only once. The rand() function produces a pseudo-random sequence of integers based on the seed value. If the program is given the same seed value each time it is run, it produces the same sequence of "random" integers. Therefore, it is common to use the system clock to set the random number seed.

### 6.7.5 TIME.H

This file contains a number of functions and definitions that can be used to access the computer system clock. Some of these are given below. Following the table, a program is presented that illustrates the use of the time functions.

**TABLE 6.4**

| | |
|---|---|
| `time_t` | A type identifier used to represent time values |
| `clock_t` | A type identifier used to represent clock values |
| `CLOCKS_PER_SEC` | A symbolic constant representing the number of processor clock cycles per second |
| `struct tm {`<br>`  int tm_sec;`<br>`  int tm_min;`<br>`  int tm_hour;`<br>`  int tm_mday;`<br>`  int tm_mon;`<br>`  int tm_year;`<br>`  int tm_wday;`<br>`  int tm_yday;`<br>`  int tm_isdst;`<br>`};` | A structure representing the time on a 24-hour clock, day of month (1 to 31), month (0 to 11), weekday (Sunday equals 0), year–1900, day of year (0 to 365), and a flag that is nonzero if daylight savings time is in effect. |
| `struct tm*localtime`<br>`(const time_t*timer);` | Returns a pointer to the structure containing 24-hour time, given `time_t`. This structure is a static that is overwritten with each call. |

```cpp
#include <time.h>
#include <iostream.h>
void main ()
{
    time_t timer;
    struct tm *tblock;

    //get time in seconds
    timer = time(NULL);

    //create a tm structure
    tblock = localtime(&timer);

    //write out date
    cout << tblock->tm_mon + 1 << "/"
         << tblock->tm_mday << "/"
         << tblock->tm_year + 1900 << "\n";

    clock_t ck = clock();

    //write out seconds elapsed since program
    //execution
    cout << ck / (double) CLOCKS_PER_SEC;
}
```

# CHAPTER 7

# Working with Character Strings

## 7.1 Character Strings

Character strings in C++ are implemented as arrays of characters. Two methods for declaring and initializing a string are illustrated below.

```
char greeting[32] = "Hello World!";
char name[] = "Joan Smith";
```

The first example allocates 32 characters for `greeting` and loads "Hello World!" starting at `greeting[0]`. Extra space is unused. The second example allocates to `name` exactly the amount of space required to store the string "Joan Smith".

C++ provides a library of string processing functions in the header file STRING.H. These are summarized in the following tables. Note that calls to the "destructive" string functions result in changes to the string specified as the first argument to the function. Consequently, these cannot be called with a `const` string as the first argument.

**TABLE 7.1**
**Nondestructive String Function Table**

| `int strcmp(char* s1, char* s2)` | Returns 0 if s1 is equal to s2, –1 if s1 is less than s2, and +1 if s1 is greater than s2. |
|---|---|
| `int strncmp(char* s1, char* s2, int n)` | Compare at most n characters in s1 and s2 |
| `int strlen(char* s)` | Returns the length of a string |
| `char* strchr(char* s, char c)` | Returns pointer to first occurrence of c in s |
| `char* strrchr(char* s, char c)` | Returns pointer to last occurrence of c in s |
| `char* strpbrk(char* s1, char* s2)` | Returns pointer to first occurrence in s1 of any of the characters that are in s2 |
| `int strspn(char* s1, char* s2)` | Return of the length of the largest prefix of s1 that consists entirely of characters in s2 |
| `int strcspn(char* s1, char* s2)` | Return the length of the largest prefix of s1 that consists entirely of characters not in s2 |

**TABLE 7.2**
**Destructive String Function Table**

| `char* strcpy(char* s1, char* s2)` | Copies s2 into s1 |
|---|---|
| `char* strncpy(char* s1, char* s2, int n)` | Copies at most n characters from s2 into s1 |
| `char* strcat(char* s1, char* s2)` | Concatenates s2 on to the end of s1 |
| `char* strncat(char* s1, char* s2, int n)` | Concatenates at most n characters from s2 onto s1 |
| `char* strtok(char* s1, char* delim)` | Break s1 into tokens (See text) |

The string library package adopts the convention of using the character '\0' to mark the end of a string. This "end of string" marker is automatically inserted and maintained by the library functions, and for most purposes the programmer need not be aware of its existence. However, it may be important to remember that every string will contain this one additional character. Thus, the variable greeting can hold at most 31 characters of data.

When comparing strings, characters from the two strings are compared in succession until the characters are not equal or until an end of string ('\0') is encountered. Similarly, when copying one string to another, successive characters are copied until the end-of-string mark in the source string is encountered. Because range checking is usually not the default, caution must be exercised when copying and comparing strings.

The strtok() function is used to process the individual *tokens* in a string. A token is a sequence of characters forming a meaningful lexical unit (a word, for example). To use strtok(), it should be called once with the first argument being the string to be processed and the second a string indicating the delimiter characters that mark the end of a token. After this call, the function will replace the first occurrence in s of a delim character with '\0' and return a pointer to the first token in s. The first time the function is called this will usually be a pointer equal to s since a string usually begins with a token.

Subsequent calls to strtok() should be made using NULL as its first argument. The function will return a pointer to the next token in s each time it is called. It will return NULL when there are no more tokens in s. The program below illustrates the use of strtok().

Also below are a few examples illustrating the workings of some of the other string functions. All functions that return pointers return NULL if they are unsuccessful.

```
#include <string.h>
#include <iostream.h>
void main()
{
  char *s = "This is it", *delim = " ", *tok;
//set up strtok for processing s
//and return pointer to first token
  tok = strtok(s, delim);
  do {
  cout << tok << '\n';
//get pointer to the next token, NULL
//if none
    tok = strtok(NULL, delim);
  } while (tok != NULL);
}
```

Program illustrating use of the strtok() function.

# CHAPTER 8

# Classes and Objects

## 8.1 Class Definition

Just as a structure definition encapsulates a set of related data items, a class definition encapsulates related data items and functions that manipulate them. A simple class definition for a `vehicle` data type is shown below:

```
class vehicle {
public:
  int wheels;
  float weight;
  void initialize(float in_weight,
                  int in_wheels = 4);
  float wheel_loading();
  void honk();
};
```

The elements defined within a class (`wheels`, `weight`, `initialize()`, etc.) are referred to as *members* of the class.

Function class members are called *methods* to distinguish them from regular functions. Typically, only the method prototypes appear within the class definition. Subsequent to the class definition, the methods would be elaborated as

```
void vehicle::initialize(float in_weight,
                         int in_wheels = 4)
{
   wheels = in_wheels;
   weight = in_weight;
}
```

The syntax `vehicle::initialize()` specifies that the specific `initialize()` method being implemented is the one included in the `vehicle` class, as opposed to some other `initialize()` method, or an `initialize()` function not associated with any class.

It is traditional to place a class definition in a header file and the implementation of its methods in a corresponding source code file. Following this practice, the vehicle class definition would be present in VEHICLE.H and its implementation in VEHICLE.CC.

It is possible to include a complete method definition within the bounds of a class definition, but doing so automatically marks the function as `inline`. Consequently, this should be done only for very small functions.

The example below shows how the `vehicle` class would be used. The components of a class variable are selected using the dot operator '`.`' just as components of a structure are selected. Class variables, such as `s1` and `s2` in the example, are called *objects* in C++. The process of selecting a method from a particular object is often described as sending a *message* to that object. Thus, the statement `s2.honk()` is interpreted as sending `s2` the `honk()` message. Objects therefore receive messages and execute their methods appropriately.

```
main ()
{
 vehicle s1, s2;
 s1.initialize(2000);
 cout << s1.wheel_loading();
 s2.initialize(25, 2);
 s2.honk();
}
```

## 8.2   The public, private, and protected Keywords

public class members are accessible from anywhere, private members are accessible only within the class itself (they are not inherited into derived classes), and protected members are accessible within the class and any of its derived classes. The creation of separate public, private, and protected sections is called *information hiding* and is a fundamental principle of object-oriented programming.

It is convenient to think of a class as defining a set of attributes and behaviors. Methods specify behaviors and variables (wheels, weight) specify attributes. Usually, the public section of a class is used to define methods only while the variables representing attributes are placed in the protected section of a class. Methods are usually provided to set and access class attributes (*accessor methods*). A modified vehicle class incorporating these principles is presented below. Since the number of wheels and base weight of a vehicle are presumably unchangeable values, only accessor methods are provided.

```
class vehicle {
public:
      void initialize(float in_weight,
                      int in_wheels = 4);
      int GetWheels()
         { return wheels; }
      int GetWeight()
         { return weight; }
      float wheel_loading();
      void honk();
protected:
      int wheels;
      float weight;
};
```

## 8.3 Specialized Methods

### 8.3.1 Constructor Methods

Because initialization methods are so common, a class definition usually specifies a *constructor* method. Constructor methods are automatically called when an object is declared. They are given the name of the class itself and must not be given a return type specification. Thus, the `initialize()` method of the `vehicle` class can be replaced with a constructor method.

```
class vehicle {
public:
  vehicle(float in_weight, int in_wheels = 4)
  {
    weight = in_weight;
    wheels = in_wheels;
  }
  //rest as before
};
```

Given this definition, statements such as `vehicle v1, v2(2000), v3(25, 2)` could be used to create vehicle objects.

A more concise syntax for constructor methods allows the parameter list of a constructor method to be followed by one or more initialization expressions of the form `variable(value)`. The syntax is illustrated below.

```
class vehicle {
public:
  vehicle(float in_weight, int in_wheels = 4) :
  weight(in_weight),
  wheels(in_wheels)
  {
  }
  //rest as before
};
```

Since C++ allows for function overloading, classes may provide several constructor methods. In fact, it is recommended that all classes provide a constructor method that takes no parameters. This is referred to as a *default* constructor.

```
class vehicle {
public:
  vehicle()
  {
    weight = 0;
    wheels = 0;
  }
  vehicle(float in_weight, int in_wheels = 4)
  {
    weight = in_weight;
    wheels = in_wheels;
  }
  //rest as before
};
```

### 8.3.2   Destructor Methods

Some data types may require action to be taken when an object of that type is deallocated. These actions can be defined in a *destructor* method. Destructor methods are identified by the class name preceded by the tilde '~' mark. For example, the destructor method for the `vehicle` class would be called `~vehicle()`. Destructor methods are needed for classes that contain dynamically allocated data structures such as linked lists or dynamic arrays but are not truly necessary for other classes. Like constructors, destructor methods should not be given a return type specification.

### 8.3.3   Copy Methods

Along with constructors and destructors, it is also common to associate *copy methods* with class types (these are called *default copy constructors* by some authors). Copy method prototypes have the form `type(const type& variable)` and specify how to construct a copy of an object. Copy methods are automatically called when, for example, an object is passed by value into a function. It is particularly important to specify copy constructors for objects that contain dynamically allocated data structures. Return types should not be specified for copy constructors.

### 8.3.4 Operator Methods

Many classes will want to provide operator methods. For example, a matrix or complex number class would presumably overload the arithmetic operators. It is customary for all classes, however, to overload the assignment operator. When defined as a method for a given class, the assignment operator has a single parameter which is a reference to an object of that class, copies that object, then returns a reference to the object being assigned to. The keyword this is used within a method definition as a pointer to the object receiving the message (the *host* object). The general form of an assignment operator method is therefore

```
class_type& operator =(const class_type& source)
{
//copy source into host object
  return *this //return a reference to the
               //object itself (not a pointer to
               //the object)
}
```

The implementation of an assignment operator method is given in the example below, where the complete definition of the vehicle class is presented.

```
class vehicle {
public:
  //constructor methods
  vehicle()
  {
    weight = 0;
    wheels = 0;
  }

  vehicle(float in_weight, int in_wheels = 4)
  {
```

```cpp
    weight = in_weight;
    wheels = in_wheels;
  }

  //copy constructor
  vehicle(const vehicle& v)
    { wheels = v.wheels; weight = v.weight; };

  //operator definitions
  vehicle& operator =(const vehicle& v)
  {
    wheels = v.wheels;
    weight = v.weight;
    return *this;
  }

  //accessor methods
  int GetWheels() { return wheels; }
  int GetWeight() { return weight; }

  //other methods
  float wheel_loading()
    { return (weight / wheels); }
  void honk() { cout << "Beep Beep!\n"; }

  //destructor method (no action required
  //because no dynamic memory)
  ~vehicle() { }
protected:
  int wheels;
  float weight;
};
```

## 8.4 `friend` Functions

Under normal circumstances, the `protected` members of a class cannot be accessed outside of that class. One way to provide an exception to this is through the `friend` mechanism. When a function or class is defined to be a `friend` of another class it has access to all of that class's members. `friend` functions are specified in a class definition by stating `friend prototype` and `friend` classes by stating `friend class_name` anywhere within the class definition. It is usual, however, to place `friend` declarations at the very top of a class definition. The technique of declaring a `friend` function is illustrated below.

```
class vehicle {
   friend void reset(vehicle, int, int);
public:
   //rest as before
};


void reset(vehicle v, int in_wheels,
            int in_weight)
{
//note access to protected members of vehicle
   v.wheels = in_wheels;
   v.weight = in_weight;
}
```

The `friend` mechanism violates the usual class access mechanism and so should be used sparingly. The example provided is not a particularly good use of the mechanism and is provided for pedagogical purposes only.

## 8.5 A Linked List Class

To tie all the various class definition features together into a single example, a program is presented in which a linked list of characters is defined. Note that pointers are used with objects in the same manner as structures.

The `ListCell` class represents a single node in a list. Each node contains a character value and a pointer to the next node in the list. The `List` class encapsulates a pointer to the first node in a list and various list manipulation functions.

The function `List::Add(char c)` creates a new `ListCell` containing c and then sets `First` to point to this new cell. The effect is to insert the new node at the beginning of the list. Note that the `List()` constructor initializes `First` to `NULL`. This ensures that the last node in a list will always have a next value of `NULL`.

```cpp
#include <iostream.h>
#define NULL 0


class List;
class ListCell {
friend List;
public:
    ListCell(char c, ListCell *p = NULL)
        : contents(c), Next(p) {}
    ListCell()
        : contents('\0'), Next(NULL) {}
    ListCell(const ListCell& lc)
    {
        contents = lc.contents;
        Next = lc.Next;
    }

    ListCell& operator =(const ListCell& lc)
    {
        contents = lc.contents;
        Next = lc.Next;
        return *this;
    }

    char GetContents() { return contents; }
    ListCell* GetNext() { return Next; }
```

```cpp
    ~ListCell() {}
protected:
    char contents;
    ListCell* Next;
};

class List {
public:
  List() { First = NULL; }

  List (const List&);
  List& operator =(List& l);

  void add(char c)
  {
    First = new ListCell(c, First);
  }

  void remove(char);
  int IsIn(char);

  ~List();
protected:
  ListCell* First;
};

List::List(const List& l)
{
if (l.First == NULL)
    First = NULL;
else
{
    First =
```

```cpp
          new ListCell(l.First->contents,
                    NULL);
      ListCell *pl = l.First->Next;
      ListCell *p2 = First;
      while (pl != NULL)
      {
      p2->Next =
      new ListCell(pl->contents,
      NULL);
      p2 = p2->Next;
      pl = pl->Next;
      }
}
}
List& List::operator =(List& l)
{
  if (l.First == NULL) return *this;
  ListCell *q = First, *next;
  while (q != Null)
  {
    next = q->Next;
    delete q;
    q = next;
  }
  First =
    new ListCell(l.First->contents,
                        NULL);
  ListCell *pl = l.First->Next;
  ListCell *p2 = First;
  while (pl != NULL)
  {
    p2->Next =
        new ListCell(pl->contents, NULL);
      p2 = p2->Next;
    pl = pl->Next;
```

```
  }
  return *this;
}

List::~List()
{
  ListCell *p = First, *next;
  while (p != NULL)
  {
    next = p->Next;
    delete p;
    p = next;
  }
}

int List::IsIn(char c)
{
  ListCell* p = First;
  while (p != NULL)
  {
    if (p->contents == c) break;
    p = p->Next;
  }
  return p != NULL;
}

void List::remove(char c)
{
  ListCell *p1 = First, *p2 = NULL;
  while (p1->contents != c)
  {
    p2 = p1;
    p1 = p1->Next;
  }
  p2->Next = p1->Next;
  delete p1;
}
```

```
void main()
{
  List l1, l2;
  l1.add('a');
  l1.add('b');
  l1.add('c');
  l2 = l1;
  l1.remove('b');
  cout << l1.IsIn('b') << l2.IsIn('c');
}
```

## 8.6   Class Nesting

The ListCell class in the previous example exists solely to aid in the implementation of the List class. It is meaningless outside of List, and programmers have no need to use it since the List class performs all the behaviors necessary for construction and manipulation of lists. Consequently, to enhance information hiding one might want to "hide" the entire ListCell class by enclosing it within the protected section of the List class. The syntax is outlined below.

```
class List {
public:
//exactly as before
protected:
 class ListCell {
  friend List;
 public:
  //exactly as before
 protected:
  //exactly as before
 };

 ListCell* First;
};
```

Because class `ListCell` is defined within the `protected` section of `List`, it is not accessible outside of `List`, but the `List` class may use it as necessary.

Classes may also be defined within the `public` section of another class. In these cases, the inner class is publicly accessible, but references to it must be qualified with the scope resolution operator. That is, if class `inner` is defined within the `public` section of class `outer`, `inner` can be referenced only by using the notation `outer::inner`.

Class nesting merely affects the scope of a class. It does not in any way modify the class member access rules. Therefore, `ListCell` must still declare class `List` as a `friend` in order to provide `List` access to its `protected` members.

If members of a nested class are not implemented `inline`, the scope resolution operator must be used twice when the method is defined.

```
class outer {
  ...
  class inner {
    int a_method();
    ...
  }
  ...
};


int outer::inner::a_method()
{
  ...
}
```

Type identifiers can also be defined within the scope of a class and either `public` or `protected` access can be provided, just as with nested classes. For example, the class below contains a publicly accessible enumerated type definition. External to the class, access to the enumerated constants must be qualified by the class name in which they are defined. The same would be true for any identifiers created by `typedef` statements within the `public` section of a class.

```
class code_table {
public:
  enum instruction {add, sub, mult,
  div, mov, cmp, jmp};
  ...
  int lookup(instruction op);
  ...
};

void main()
{
  code_table c;
  int i = c.lookup(code_table::mult);
}
```

## 8.7    `static` Members

Normally, every instance of a class contains individual instances of the class member attributes. For example, every `vehicle` object has individual `weight` and `wheels` variables. However, a class member that is declared as `static` is shared among all the instances of the class. Only one copy of a `static` class member exists regardless of how many instances of the class have been created.

`static` class members are often used to store data that is shared among all instances of a class. In these cases duplicating the data in every object is wasteful. `static` members are also useful when there is information that must be communicated to all instances of a class—for example, a condition flag or a counter variable.

`static` member variables are declared within a class but must be explicitly allocated by a declaration statement with file level scope. For example, in VEHICLE.H one would write:

```
class vehicle {
public:
  ...
```

```
protected:
  static int number_of_vehicles;
};
```

While in VEHICLE.CPP one would write:

```
#include "vehicle.h"

int vehicle::number_of_vehicles = 0;

vehicle::vehicle()
{
  number_of_vehicles = number_of_vehicles + 1;
  ...
}
```

## 8.8   Type Conversion Methods

The code below defines a fraction class. The function overloading facility is used to provide several different constructor functions, and the multiplication operator is overloaded for fractions.

```
class fraction {
public:
  fraction(int top, int bot) :
    numerator(top), denominator(bot) {}
  fraction(int top) :
    numerator(top), denominator(1) {}
  fraction() :
    numerator(0), denominator(1) {}
protected:
  int numerator, denominator;
};


fraction operator *(fraction& fl,
```

```
                    fraction& f2)
{
   return fraction(f1.top()*f2.top(),
                   f1.bot()*f2.bot());
}
```

The constructor `fraction(int)` describes how to construct a fraction given an integer. It can also serve as a function for converting integers to fractions. In fact, it will be automatically used in this manner whenever the need arises, as in the sequence below.

```
fraction f1(2,3), f2;
f2 = f1 * 2; //f2 is now 4/3
```

In this example, the operand 2 is automatically converted to the fraction 2/1 using the `fraction(int)` constructor. Fraction multiplication is then performed. This constructor would also be invoked in the following situation:

```
void fn(fraction f)
{
   ... //do something
}

void main()
{
   int i;
   ...
   fn(i); //i will be converted to a
          //fraction and fn() invoked
   ...
}
```

In this manner, constructor methods for a given class serve as functions that convert from some other class to that class.

It is also possible to specify type conversion in the opposite direction. For example, one may wish the system to be able to convert automatically from fractions to decimals. This can be accomplished by adding the following method to the `fraction` class:

```
class fraction {
public:
    ...
    operator float()
    {
      return (float) numerator /
             (float) denominator;
    };
protected:
    ...
};
```

A method of the form `class::operator type()` specifies an algorithm for converting a class object into a value of the specified type. In this case, a fraction is converted to a decimal by performing floating-point division on the numerator and denominator. Given this method, the following sequence can be performed:

```
fraction f1(2,3);
float x;
x = f1 + 0.2; //x is 0.866667
```

The automatic type conversions that one can create in C++ are a great convenience, but can also result in ambiguous expressions like the one below.

```
fraction f1(2,3), f2;
f2 = f1 * 2; //ambiguous conversion
```

The second statement is ambiguous because the compiler is unable to decide whether to perform floating-point or fraction multiplication. The solution is to use explicit type casting:

```
f2 = f1 * (fraction) 2;
```

# CHAPTER 9

# Inheritance

## 9.1 Simple Inheritance

The inheritance mechanism allows a programmer to derive a new class type from an existing class type. Classes so created are called *derived* classes. The classes they are derived from are called *base* classes. For example, one may define a truck class to be a specific kind of vehicle.

```
class truck : public vehicle {
public:
  truck(float in_weight,
        int in_wheels = 4,
        float max_load = 24000.0)
  {
    wheels = in_wheels;
    weight = in_weight;
    payload = max_load;
  }

  float efficiency()
  { return payload / (payload + weight); }
```

```
  void honk()
  { cout << "Aooga!\n" }
protected:
  float payload;
};
```

The syntax `public vehicle` means that the `truck` class will inherit the variables and methods defined in the `vehicle` class. Thus, a `truck` object will have `wheels`, `weight`, and `payload` attributes, and `wheel_loading()`, `efficiency()`, and `honk()` methods. Just as a truck is derived from the `vehicle` class, one could similarly define other derived classes of `vehicle`, derived classes of those derived classes, and so on, forming a hierarchy of data types.

Destructor, constructor, copy, and assignment methods are not inherited to derived classes and must be explicitly created if they are desired.

It is frequently useful for derived classes to redefine a method or attribute that it is present in one of its base classes. A `truck`, for example, has a distinctive `honk()` method. When a `truck` object receives a `honk()` message it will respond by displaying "Aooga!" since that is the message specifically associated with trucks. Instances of other `vehicle` classes that do not have specific `honk()` methods would respond by displaying "Beep Beep!" when receiving a `honk()` message. In general, when an object receives a message, it will search up through its inheritance hierarchy until it finds a matching method, then execute that method.

## 9.2 Construction and Destruction of Derived Class Objects

An alternate way of defining the `truck()` constructor method would involve first invoking the `vehicle` constructor, then performing any construction steps specific to `truck`. The method definition below adopts this approach to `truck` construction.

```
truck(float in_weight,
      int in_wheels = 4,
      float max_load = 24000.0) :
vehicle(in_weight, in_wheels)
```

```
{
   payload = max_load;
}
```

The notation : `base class(arg1, arg2 ...)` following a constructor invokes the base constructor with the specified arguments.

If the base class constructor is not explicitly called in this way, the C++ compiler will automatically generate a call to the base class's default constructor (the constructor with no parameters) before the derived class's constructor is called. If the base class has no default constructor, the derived class will not compile. Thus, when a derived class object is created, the various relevant constructor methods are executed beginning with the topmost base class and proceeding down the inheritance hierarchy for each class on the inheritance path.

When a derived class object is destroyed, class destructors are automatically executed in the reverse order in which the constructors were executed.

## 9.3   Inheritance and Information Hiding

The keywords can be used to control the inheritance mechanism when derived classes are created. As seen in the previous section, the usual method of specifying class derivation is to specify `public base_class` in the derived class definition. Using this technique, called `public` derivation, the `public` members of the base class become `public` members of the derived class and the `protected` members of the base class become `protected` members of the derived class. (`private` members are never inherited.)

One may also specify `protected` or `private` derivation by writing `protected base_class` or `private base_class` after the derived class name. When `protected` derivation is used, the `public` and `protected` members of the base class become `protected` members of the derived class. Under `private` derivation, the `public` and `protected` members of the base class become `private` members of the derived class.

## 9.4 Multiple Inheritance

It is possible for a class to be derived from more than one base class. This situation is called multiple inheritance and is illustrated by the example below.

```
class rental_car : public vehicle {
public:
  rental_car(float in_rate,
             float in_weight,
             int in_wheels = 4) :
  vehicle(in_weight, in_wheels)
  {
    daily_rate = in_rate;
  }
  float rate() { return daily_rate; }
protected:
  float daily_rate;
};


class driver {
public:
  driver(float in_rate) { hourly_rate = in_rate; }
  float rate() { return hourly_rate; }
protected:
  float hourly_rate;
};


class chauffeured_vehicle : public rental_car,
                            public driver {
public:
  chauffeured_vehicle(float vehicle_rate,
               float driver_rate,
               float in_weight,
               int in_wheels = 4) :
```

```
rental_car(vehicle_rate, in_weight, in_wheels),
driver(driver_rate)
{}

float cost(float hours)
{
    return hourly_rate*hours +
        ((int)(hours/24+0.5))*daily_rate;
}
};
```

In this example, the `chauffeured_vehicle` class is derived from both `rental_car` and `driver`. Any `chauffeured_vehicle` object contains all the methods and attributes of `vehicle`, `rental_car`, `driver`, and `chauffeured_vehicle`.

When multiple inheritance occurs it is easily possible for the same identifier to be present in two or more of a class's base classes. In the example above, the `chauffeured_vehicle` class inherits a `rate()` method from both its base classes. Given `cv` as a `chauffeured_vehicle` object, the reference `cv.rate()` is therefore ambiguous. The scope resolution operator is used to resolve the ambiguous references in these cases. Using this operator, one could access `cv.rental_car::rate()` or `cv.driver::rate()`.

Similar syntax is used to resolve ambiguous references to base class components within a class definition. For example, the `cost()` method could be written as:

```
float cost(float hours)
{ return driver::rate()*hours +
((int)(hours/24+0.5))*
rental_car::rate();
}
```

## 9.5 `virtual` Methods and Polymorphism

Given the declaration vehicle  *p, it is acceptable for p to point to either a vehicle object or a truck object since truck objects are derived from the vehicle class. Since vehicle and truck have different honk() methods, one would presumably like the expression p->honk() to display either "Beep! Beep!" or "Aooga" depending upon the class of object p is pointing to. This desired behavior is called *polymorphism*.

However, by default, methods in C++ do *not* exhibit polymorphic behavior. Thus, if p is a pointer to a vehicle, and given the class definitions of vehicle and truck seen earlier, the invocation p->honk() will always result in the execution of vehicle::honk() even if p happens to point to a truck object. To produce polymorphic behavior in a method, a C++ programmer must mark that method as being virtual, as shown below.

```
class vehicle {
public:
  virtual void honk()
    { cout << "Beep Beep!\n"; }
};


class truck : public vehicle {
 public:
 virtual void honk()
    { cout << "Aooga! \n"; }
};
```

The invocation of virtual methods requires a great deal of run time overhead that is not required for invoking normal methods. This is why methods are not virtual by default. Programmers should consider carefully which methods require polymorphism and which do not. Only those methods that require it should be marked as virtual.

The keyword virtual should appear only within a class definition. That is, if only the method's prototype is given in the class definition, the prototype should be marked as virtual but the implementation should not be. This is illustrated here:

```
class vehicle {
public:
  ...
//declare virtual in prototype
  virtual void honk();
  ...
protected:
  ...
};


//do not repeat the virtual keyword here
void vehicle::honk()
{
  cout << "Beep! Beep!";
}
```

## 9.6   Abstract Classes

A *pure* `virtual` *method* is defined using the notation:

`    virtual type name(arg1, arg2 ...) = 0;`

A class with one or more pure `virtual` methods is called an *abstract* class. No objects of that class can be created. Abstract classes can only be used as a base class for another class. They are often used to create *schemas* which define a set of related classes.

```
class shape {
public:
  ...
  virtual draw() = 0;
  ...
};


class square : public shape {
public:
  ...
```

```
virtual draw();  //square class MUST implement
                 //this method since it is a pure
                 //function in its base class
    ...
};
```

# CHAPTER 10

# Templates

## 10.1  Class Templates

Templates allow for the creation of generic program constructs. As the name suggests, templates do not define executable code, but define a form from which code can be generated. Templates must be *instantiated* to create usable program units (classes, functions, and so forth).

A template has the form template<parameters> construct. For example, the following defines a template for a class named vector. In this example, t is a template parameter that represents the data type that is to be stored in the vector. The term "class" is somewhat misleading here. In this context, class means any C++ data type.

```
template<class t>
class vector {
public:
 vector(){contents = NULL;}
 vector(int in_size) : size(in_size)
    { contents = new t[size]; }
 vector(int in_size, t initial_value);
 ~vector() { delete[] contents; }
```

```
//return reference to specified element
  t& operator [](int index);
protected:
  int size;
  t *contents;
};


//note that each method implementation must be
//preceded by its own template statement

template<class t>
vector<t>::vector(int in_size,
              t initial_value)
  : size(in_size)
{
 contents = new t[size];
 for (int i = 0; i <= size-1; ++i)
    contents[i] = initial_value;
}


template<class t>
t& vector<t>::operator [](int index)
{
 assert((index >= 0) && (index <= size));
 return contents[index];
}
```

The template is used to generate particular vector classes by specifying
vector<type> in a declaration where type is a type identifier specifying
the type of value to be stored in the vector. This notation causes the template
to be instantiated for that particular type, in effect causing the compiler to generate a class definition by replacing the template parameter with the specified
type identifier. The method is illustrated in the example shown.

```
void main()
```

```
{
//a is a vector of integers
vector<int> a(100);
//b is a vector of floats
vector<float> b(50);
...
}
```

Since it is tedious to write vector<type> whenever a vector is declared, it is common practice to use a typedef statement to associate type identifiers with template instantiations, as shown below.

```
typedef vector<int> int_vector;
typedef vector<float> float_vector;
...
void main()
{
   int_vector a(100);
  float_vector b(50);
  ...
}
```

Since templates are definitions only and do not themselves cause object code to be generated, they should be placed in header files when used as part of a larger program. That is, in the case of the vector template, both the class specification and the method implementations should be placed in the header file.

A template identifier (vector for example) can never be written without the required template parameters. This is because there is no class called vector. Rather, vector is an outline from which a class can be generated. Therefore, in writing the implementation of the vector methods, it is necessary to write vector<t>::operator [](int index) and precede this by a statement specifying the template parameters.

Templates are very convenient, but programmers must be careful when using them. They may not be as generic as they seem. For example, the vector template will instantiate correctly only for data types for which the assignment operator is defined. This is because the assignment operator is used with a t type variable in the implementation of the "initial value" constructor method.

Since the assignment operator will not work with arrays, the following sequence would not compile:

```
typedef float matrix[100][100];
typedef vector<matrix, 50> //ERROR!
```

Should one wish to do this, the assignment operator must first be overloaded to work with matrix types.

## 10.2   Function Templates

Templates can also be used to write generic functions. For example, one could define a generic sort() function template:

```
template<class t>
void sort(t *a, int size)
{
  ...
  //insert your favorite sorting
  //algorithm here
  ...
}
```

The C++ compiler is intelligent enough to automatically instantiate a function template when it encounters a template function call. Thus, given the template above, the following code sequence would be permissible:

```
int a[100];
float x[50];
...
//put some values in the arrays
...
sort(a, 100);
sort(x, 50);
```

The compiler realizes that the call sort(a, 100) requires an instantiation of sort<int> and does so automatically. Similarly, the call sort(x, 50) causes an instantiation of the sort<> template with parameter float.

Function templates can have the same sort of hidden dependencies that class templates can have. For example, just as the vector<> template works only for classes for which assignment is defined, the sort<> template would presumably only work for data types for which the relevant comparison operator is defined ('<' or '>' depending upon how the sort is implemented).

## 10.3  Templates for Derived Classes

In order to illustrate the use of templates with derived classes, a subclass of vector is defined below which allows for the programmer to specify upper and lower bounds for the vector's indices.

```
template<class t>
class indexed_vector : public vector<t> {
public:
  indexed_vector() : upper(0), lower(0) {}
  indexed_vector(int first, int last) :
  vector<t>(last-first+1)
  {
    upper = first;
    lower = last;
  }


  indexed_vector(int first, int last, t value) :
  vector<t>(last-first+1, value)
  {
    upper = first;
    lower = last;
  }


  t& operator [](int index)
  {
    return vector<t>::operator [](index - lower);
  }
protected:
```

```
int upper, lower;
};
```

## 10.4 Templates for Recursive Classes

The code below illustrates the use of templates in creating recursive structures, in this case the List class seen earlier. Readers should again note that wherever a class name is required, a template parameter must be provided. A typedef is used in List to avoid the necessity of writing ListCell<t> whenever a reference to that class is needed.

```
template<class t>
class ListCell;

template<class t>
class ListCell {
  friend List<t>;
public:
  ListCell(t c, ListCell<t> *p = NULL)
    : contents(c), Next(p) {}

  ListCell<t>& operator =
    (const ListCell<t>& lc)
  {
    contents = lc.contents;
    Next = lc.Next;
    return *this;
  }

  t GetContents()
    { return contents; }
  ListCell<t>* GetNext()
    { return Next; }
```

```cpp
  ~ListCell() {}
protected:
  t contents;
  ListCell<t>* Next;
};


template<class t>
class List {
  typedef ListCell<t> tCell;
public:
  List() { First = NULL; }

  List (const List<t>&);
  List<t>& operator =(List<t>& l)

  void add(t c)
    { First = new tCell(c, First); }
  void remove(t);
  int IsIn(t);

  ~List();
protected:
  tCell* First;
};


template<class t>
List<t>::List(const List<t>& l)
{
  if (l.First == NULL)
    First = NULL;
  else
  {
    First = new tCell(l.First->contents, NULL);
```

```
   tCell *p1 = l.First->Next;
   tCell *p2 = First;
   while (p1 != NULL)
   {
    cout << p1->contents;
    p2->Next = new tCell(p1->contents, NULL);
    p2 = p2->Next;
    p1 = p1->Next;
   }
 }
}

//and so on for other List<t> methods
```

# CHAPTER 11

# Input and Output

## 11.1 Files and Streams

Input and output facilities are provided by the functions and objects defined within the IOSTREAM.H file, included with every C++ implementation. Programmers may also opt to perform I/O using the C library package, STDIO.H, but this usage is archaic and is not discussed here.

The IOSTREAM.H file provides access to standard input via the `cin` object, standard output via the `cout` object, and to the standard error device via `cerr`. The insertion operator '`<<`' is used to write to `cout` or `cerr`, and the extraction operator '`>>`' is used to read from `cin`. Their use is illustrated below.

```
cout << "Please enter two integer values\n";
cin >> i >> j;
cout << "You entered " << i <<
    << j << " \nTheir sum is "
    << i + j << '\n';
```

The object `cin` skips over all white space (blanks, tabs, and newlines) when performing a '`>>`' operation. When reading an integer, it consumes a sign, if present, then consumes characters until a non-digit is encountered. Real numbers are read in an analogous manner. Some examples are presented in the table below. The table assumes i is an integer, x is a decimal, and c is a character.

The objects `cin`, `cout`, and `cerr` are all instances of the class `iostream`. In addition to the `<<` and `>>` stream operators, there are a number of methods defined for `iostream` objects. These are summarized in Table 11.2.

The `width()` method can be used to set the output field width for `cout`. When the width is zero, as it is by default, values are printed with no leading spaces. If the width is set to a number larger than the number of digits to be written, the value is padded with the current fill character. The fill character is a space by default and may be set using the `fill()` method. Note that when the width is set using the `width()` method it affects only the next output item. Afterward, the width automatically resets to zero.

## TABLE 11.1
### Examples Showing Effect of >> with `cin`

| Input source | Effect of `cin >> i >> c >>x` |
|---|---|
| 123 a123 | i = 123 <br> c = 'a' <br> x = 123.0 |
| 123 <br> a <br> 123.5 | i = 123 <br> c = 'a' <br> x = 123.5 |
| +123a.123 | i = 123 <br> c = 'a' <br> x = 0.123 |
| 123aa123 | i = 123 <br> c = 'a' <br> x is undefined due to unexpected input |
| a123 c123 | all variables undefined due to unexpected input when reading i |

## TABLE 11.2
## Methods for `iostream` Objects

| | |
|---|---|
| `char get()` | Read and return the next character, including whitespace characters |
| `put(char c)` | Output c |
| `read(char s[], int size)` | Read size number of characters and put them in s |
| `write(char s[],int size)` | Write size number of character from s |
| `get_line(char s[], int n, char delim = '\n');` | Read at most n-1 characters until the delim character or eof is encountered. Put them in s, followed by the '\0' character |
| `width(int i)` | Set the output field width of obj to i |
| `precision(int i)` | Set the output precision of obj to i. This is the number of digits placed to the right of the decimal point. |
| `char fill(char c)` | Set the fill character to c |
| `int eof()` | Return true if obj has attempted to read past the end of the file |
| `int bad()` | Return true if an illegal operation has been requested |
| `int fail()` | Return true if obj.bad() or if an operation has failed |
| `int good()` | Return true if none of the previous error conditions apply |

Precision refers to the number of digits to print to the right of the decimal point. It is relevant only for `float` or `double` values. A number will be rounded to fit within the specified precision.

The `fail()` method is useful for testing if an operation was successful. In the example below it is used to determine if an integer was input properly.

```
cout << "Enter number of students";
cin >> n;
while (cin.fail())
{
 cout << "Try again please:";
```

```
cin >> n;
}
```

In the example below, eof(), get(), and put() are used to copy an input source. Note that eof() does not become true until after a "read past end of file" operation has been attempted.

```
char c = cin.get();
while (! cin.eof())
{
 cout.put();
 c = cin.get();
}
```

## 11.2 Overloading the Stream Operators

It is common practice for C++ programmers to overload the << and >> operators when creating new data types. For example, given the student_record structure presented earlier, one would like to be able to produce code like that shown below.

```
student_record r = {1234, 's', 3.25};
...
cout << s;
```

Doing so requires that the stream operators be overloaded to work with student_record structures. The technique is shown below.

```
ostream& operator <<(ostream& out,
                     student_record& s)
{
  out << s.id << '\t' << s.classification << '\t'
      << s.gpa << '\n';
  return out;
}
```

When overloaded, the iostream operators << and >> should always return a reference to their left operand. This, and the fact that they are left associative, ensures that they can continue to be used in the manner of a stream.

That is, given cout << a << b << c, left associativity ensures that the expression is evaluated as (((cout << a) << b) << c). The fact that << yields a reference to its left operand, cout, ensures that after evaluating (cout << a) the expression effectively becomes ((cout << b) << c), and evaluation continues in the desired manner.

## 11.3   Setting Format Options

Detailed formatting options for iostream objects can be controlled using the setf() method. This method modifies a set of bit-flags (stored within a long variable) used by iostream objects to maintain the current state of their formatting options. The ios class defines constants that can be used in conjunction with setf() to access these bit fields. These constants are presented in the table on the next page.

When called with one parameter, setf() has the effect of turning "on" the specified formatting option. When called with two parameters, the options specified by the second parameter are turned "off," then the options specified by the first parameter are turned on. For example, the statement cout.setf(ios::fixed,ios::floatfield) causes the ios::scientific flag to be turned off and the ios::fixed flag to be turned on. All real numbers are subsequently displayed in fixed-point notation. The second argument is necessary to ensure that ios::scientific will be off, since both this and ios::fixed cannot be on at the same time. Similarly, the statement cout.setf(ios::right, ios::adjustfield) would be used to set output formatting to right justification. Note that the basefield flags affect only integer output.

## TABLE 11.3
## Format Flag Constants

| | |
|---|---|
| `ios::skipws` | skip whitespace |
| `ios::left` | left justify |
| `ios::right` | right justify |
| `ios::internal` | pad after sign or base indicator |
| `ios::dec` | decimal output |
| `ios::oct` | octal output |
| `ios::hex` | hex output |
| `ios::showbase` | show base of output |
| `ios::showpoint` | force display of decimal point (decimals only) |
| `ios::uppercase` | always display in upper case |
| `ios::showpos` | add '+' to front of positive numbers |
| `ios::scientific` | displays decimals in scientific notation |
| `ios::fixed` | displays decimals in fixed point notation |
| `ios::unitbuf` | flush all streams after insertion |
| `ios::stdio` | flush `stdout`, `stderr` after insertion |
| `ios::basefield` | This is equal to:<br>`ios::dec` \| `ios::oct` \| `ios::hex` |
| `ios::adjustfield` | This is equal to:<br>`ios::left` \| `ios::right` \| `ios::internal` |
| `ios::floatfield` | This is equal to:<br>`ios::scientific` \| `ios::fixed` |

Format flags can be combined using bitwise OR to create groups of formatting options. Thus, the call `cout.setf(ios::fixed | ios::showpos | ios::uppercase, ios::floatfield)` turns off `ios::scientific` and turns on `ios::fixed`, `ios::showpos`, and `ios::uppercase`.

Because most I/O operations are buffered, it is not always possible to rely upon the fact that, for example, a message will be displayed exactly when it is written to `cout`. Instead, on many systems, output is not written to the appropriate device until the output buffer is full. The `ios::unitbuf` flag allows the programmer to specify that all I/O buffers are to be emptied as soon as an item is inserted into them. The flag `ios::stdio` restricts this to only the `cout` and `cerr` buffers.

# 11.4 Formatting and Using I/O Manipulators

In addition to using `setf()`, formatting options can be controlled by including I/O *manipulators* in a stream. These are defined in the standard header file IOMANIP.H and summarized in the table below. Manipulators have the same effects as their corresponding `iostream` methods. An example illustrating their use is given in the following table:

**TABLE 11.4**

**I/O Manipulators Defined in IOMANIP.H**

| | |
|---|---|
| `oct` | Set output base to octal |
| `dec` | Set output base to decimal |
| `hex` | Set output base to hexidecimal |
| `endl` | send '\n' and flush stream |
| `ends` | send '\0' and flush stream |
| `flush` | flush stream |
| `ws` | ignore whitespace |
| `setbase(int)` | set output base to specified integer (8, 10, or 16) |
| `setfill(char)` | set fill character |
| `setw(int)` | set output width |
| `setprecision(int)` | set output precision |
| `resetiosflags(long)` | turn off specified `ios` flags |
| `setiosflags(long)` | turn on specified `ios` flags |

The following is a program illustrating use of I/O manipulators.

```
#include <iostream.h>
#include <iomanip.h>

void main()
{
 cout
   << resetiosflags(ios::floatfield |
                     ios::adjustfield)
   << setiosflags(ios::fixed | ios::right)
   << setw(10) << setprecision(2)
   //output will now be right justified, floats
   //printed in fixed fields
     << 123.456 << endl
   //output is: 123.46
     << hex << 16 << endl
   //output is: 10
     << setw(10) << setfill('#') << 123 << endl
   //output is: ########7b
     << 123.456;
   //output is: 123.46
}
```

## 11.5  File Classes

The header file FSTREAM.H defines three file classes: ifstream, ofstream, and fstream. These are used for read-only files, write-only files, and readable-writable files, respectively. The open() and close() methods are used to associate and disassociate physical files with file objects. This is illustrated by the example below, which copies one file to another.

```
ifstream infile;
ofstream outfile;
infile.open("infile.txt");
outfile.open("outfile.txt");
char c = infile.get();
```

```
while (!infile.eof())
{
  outfile.put(c);
  c = infile.get();
}
infile.close();
outfile.close();
```

Alternately, the file name for a file object can be specified as an argument to its constructor. Thus, one could also have written:

```
ifstream infile("infile.txt");
ofstream outfile("outfile.txt");
char c = infile.get();
...
```

Objects of class fstream may be used as either read files, write files, or readable-writable files. When creating an fstream object, one of the three file modes must be specified using the constants ios::in, ios::out, or ios::in | ios::out, as illustrated below.

```
fstream read_only_file("infile.txt",
                       ios::in);
fstream write_only_file("outfile.txt",
                        ios::out);
fstream read_write_file("update.txt",
                        ios::in | ios::out);
```

One may also open a file in *append* mode by specifying ios::app.

The file classes maintain a file position marker that indicates the character position where the next I/O operation is to be performed. The methods seekp() and seekg() are used to modifiy this position marker for write and read files, respectively. The methods take two parameters. The first specifies an offset and the second specifies a starting point. Usually the second parameter is one of the values ios::beg, ios::end, ios::cur, which represent the beginning of the file, end of the file, and the current file position, respectively. Thus, given that infile is an object of type ifstream, the call infile.seekg(-1, ios::cur) has the effect of moving the file position marker back one character. Similarly, given that `outfile` is an `ofstream` object, the statement `outfile.seekp(0,ios::beg)` places the file position marker at the beginning of the file associated with `outfile`. The methods `tellp()` and `tellg()` can be used to determine the current file position marker specified as an offset from `ios::beg`.

The program below modifies a file by replacing all periods with exclamation marks.

```
#include <iostream.h>
#include <fstream.h>

void main()
{
  char fname[32];
  cout << "Enter file name: ";
  cin >> fname;
  fstream f(fname, ios::in | ios::out);
  char c = f.get();
  while (! f.eof())
  {
    if (c == '.')
    {
     f.seekp(-1, ios::cur);
     f.put('!');
    }
    c = f.get();
  }
}
```

## 11.6   Binary I/O

The preceding examples operated upon files by reading and writing individual characters. It is often convenient to read or write an entire sequence of bytes, for example a `vehicle` object or a `student_record` structure, in one operation. The `read()` and `write()` methods are used for this purpose.

These methods take two parameters: the first is an address specifying the location of the object to be read or written and the second is an integer indicating the size of the object. The address parameter should be specified using the type cast unsigned char*. For example, the sequence below writes the binary image of a vehicle object into a file.

```
ofstream ofile("vehicles");
vehicle v(2000);
ofile.write((unsigned char*) &f,
            sizeof(vehicle));
```

# CHAPTER 12

# Miscellaneous C++ Topics

## 12.1  Command Line Arguments

Although none of the previous examples has done so, it is possible for C++ main() functions to specify parameters that correspond to the command line arguments specified when the C++ program is executed. Two parameters are required to access command line arguments. The first should be an integer called argc which represents the number of command line arguments specified. The second is an array of character strings called argv. This array will be initialized by the operating system so that argv[0] is the name of the command invoked (i.e., the name of the program as specified on the command line) argv[1] is the first command line argument, arg[2] the second command line argument, and so forth. For example, consider the program below.

```
#include <iostream.h>
void main(int argc, char *argv[])
{
 cout << "Command invoked was: "
      << argv[0];
 cout << "Command line parameters were:\n";
 for (int i = 1; i <= argc; ++i)
  cout << argv[i] << '\n';
}
```

Assuming this program was compiled into the executable file test, the command test one two three would result in the following output:

```
Command invoked was: test
Command line parameters were:
one
two
three
```

## 12.2   Functions with a Variable Number of Arguments

C++ allows the specification of functions which take a variable number of arguments, provided that at least one fixed argument is provided. The notation

```
type name(type arg1, ...)
```

specifies a function that takes at least one argument. The ellipses notation specifies that a variable number of arguments may be specified following the previous arguments.

Some means of identifying the number of arguments sent to a function must be provided by the programmer. Two means are traditionally adopted. Either the function is designed so that its first parameter is the number of arguments that will be specified, or the argument list is terminated by a special value indicating the end of the argument list. Both means are used in the examples to follow.

A set of macros defined in the file STDARG.H provides the means for accessing the arguments sent to such a function with a variable number of arguments. These macros are summarized in the following table.

TABLE 12.1

**Macros**

| | |
|---|---|
| `va_list` | Used to define a pointer to the argument list provided to a function |
| `va_start(va_list, lastfix)` | Used to initialize the argument list for processing. `lastfix` should be the name of the last fixed argument provided to the function. |
| `va_arg(va_list, type)` | Used to get the next argument |
| `va_end(va_list)` | Used to "clean up" the argument list after it has been processed |

The technique used for accessing the argument list is the same in both functions. First, a variable representing the argument list is declared using the `va_list` macro. Next, the argument list is initialized for processing by calling the `va_start` macro. The first parameter to this macro should be the argument list pointer variable and the second should be the name of the last fixed argument provided to the function. After `va_start` has been executed, each successive argument is accessed using `va_arg`. Each time this is called it returns the "next" argument. The function `max1()` stops calling `va_arg` when it has processed the required number of arguments, while `max2()` stops when it encounters an argument of zero.

The second parameter to `va_arg` should be the type of the current argument. This is so that it knows how far to advance the argument pointer so that it points to the next argument. In the examples provided, all arguments are of type `int`. However, should one wish to design a function in which the number as well as types of arguments may vary, considerable complication will result.

```
#include <iostream.h>
#include <stdarg.h>

int max1(int argcnt, ... )
//function to select maximum of set of integer
//arguments.
//argcnt specifies number of arguments
{
//arguments points to argument list
```

```
 va_list arguments;
//setup for argument list processing
 va_start(arguments, argcnt);

//current_max is first of the variable
//arguments
 int next_arg;
 int current_max = va_arg(arguments, int);

//process remaining arguments
 for (int i = 1; i <= argcnt-1; ++i)
 {
    //get next argument
    next_arg = va_arg(arguments, int);
    if (next_arg > current_max)
      current_max = next_arg;
 }
 return current_max;
}


int max2(int arg1, ...)
//function to select maximum of set of integers
arguments terminated by 0
{
 va_list arguments;
 va_start(arguments, arg1);
 int next_arg = arg1;
 int current_max = arg1;

//process remaining arguments
 while (next_arg != 0)
 {
    if (next_arg > current_max)
```

```
    current_max = next_arg;
   next_arg = va_arg(arguments, int);
 }
 return current_max;
}


void main()
{
 cout << max1(3, 4, 5, 2) << '\t'
      << max1(2,4,3) << '\t'
      << max1(5, 1, 3, 4, 1, 2);
 //output will be: 544
 cout << max2(4, 5, 2, 0) << '\t'
      << max2(4,3,0) << '\t'
      << max2(1, 3, 4, 1, 2, 0);
 //output will be: 544
}
```

Program illustrating use of variable argument lists in C++

## 12.3 Function Pointers

The statement,

```
int (*int_fn)(int, int);
```

defines int_fn as a pointer to a function that takes two integer arguments
and returns an integer value. Given some function fitting that description such
as,

```
int max(int a, int b)
{
 if (a > b)
  return a;
 else
  return b;
}
```

`int_fn` can be made to point to the `max()` function by the statement `int_fn = &max`. Alternately, one may omit the address operator, so that the statement `int_fn = max` has the same effect. To execute the function pointed to by `int_fn` one writes a statement such as:

```
cout << (*int_fn)(5, 10).
```

In general, the notation `return_type (*name)(type, type, ...)` defines name to be a pointer to a function of the specified `return_type` that takes parameters of the specified number and type. The function is called using the notation

```
(*name)(arg, arg, ...).
```

The `typedef` statement is often useful when using pointers to functions. Thus, rather than having to continually repeat `int (*name)(int, int)` every time one wished to define a pointer to this sort of function, one could create a type identifier called `int_fn` to represent "pointers to integer functions that take two integer parameters":

```
typedef int (*int_fn)(int, int);
```

Or,

```
typedef float (*float_fn)(float)
```

to represent "pointers to float functions that take a single float parameter."

Pointers to functions are used most often when a function needs the name of a function as a parameter. This is illustrated below.

```
float poly1(float x)
{
  return x*x + 2*x + 1;
}


float poly2(float x)
{
  return x*x*x + 3*x*x * 4;
}


void chart(float_fn fn, float start,
           float end, float inc)
```

```
{
for(float x = start; x <= end;
    x = x + inc)
   cout << x << fn(x) << '\n';
}

  void main()
{
  chart(&poly1, 0.0, 1.0, 0.1);
  chart(&poly2, 0.0, 1.0, 0.1);
}
```

One can envision functions similar to chart() that compute the area under the curve of a specified polynomial for a specified interval, or a function that plots a given polynomial on a graphics device.

## 12.4  Exception Handling

The keyword try defines a block of code in which errors can be intercepted and processed by programmer-specified exception handling routines, specified by the keyword catch. The general form of a catch-try code segment is outlined below.

```
try {
//do something
}
catch (exception-object) {
//handle this type of exception
}
catch (exception-object) {
//handle this type of exception
}
//more catch blocks as needed
```

When an error is detected in the try block, an exception object of the appropriate class is *thrown* using the throw operator. Control is then transferred to the nearest catch block that is specified as catching that class of exception object. If no such catch block can be found, the program terminates in the usual manner.

The nearest catch block is located by back-tracking through the sequence of function calls that led to the function in which the throw statement was executed. After the catch block is executed, control is transferred to the next statement at the end of all related catch blocks, rather like executing a break statement within a switch construct. The technique is illustrated below.

```cpp
class MathErr {
public:
 MathErr(char *s) { strcpy(msg, s); }
 char msg[80];
};

class IOErr {
public:
 MathErr(char *s) { strcpy(msg, s); }
  char msg[80];
};

void io_stuff()
{
 ofstream outfile("out.txt");
 if (outfile.fail())
    throw(IOErr("File open error"));
 //do something
 outfile.close();
}

void math_stuff()
{
  float x, y;
  cin >> x >> y;
```

```
  if (y == 0)
     throw(MathErr("Divide by zero"));
  cout << x / y;
  io_stuff();
}


void main()
{
//any error outside of try block causes
//program termination in the default manner
try {
  //MathErr or IOErr objects that are "thrown"
  //will cause control to jump to
  //the appropriate catch block below
  math_stuff();
 }
 catch (MathErr& merror) {
  cout << "Program aborted due to math error: "
       << merror.msg << '\n';
 }
 catch (IOErr& ioerror) {
  cout << "Program aborted due to IO error: "
       << ioerror.msg << '\n';
 }
//control is transferred here after any of the
//above catch blocks are executed
 }
```

## 12.5  String Streams

The file STRSTREAM.H provides facilities that allow programmers to treat character strings as input and output streams. It defines two classes: ostrstream and istrstream. The former is used to write to strings, the latter to read from strings. Their use is illustrated here.

```
#include <iostream.h>
#include <strstream.h>

void main()
{
  char obuf[32];
  int i = 42;
  ostrstream ostr(obuf, 32);
  ostr << "The value of i is " << i;
//obuf is now the string "The value of i
//is 42";
  cout << obuf;
  char ibuf* = "1234";
  istrstream istr(ibuf, 4);
  istr >> i; //i is now 1234
  cout << i;
}
```

## 12.6  The void* Type

The void* type is designed to be compatible with any pointer type. void pointers cannot be referenced without explicit type casting. They pointers are usually used to specify function parameters that represent machine addresses. The example below uses the void* data type to implement a function that copies a block of memory.

void pointers are considered archaic by most authors and should be avoided if possible. Most problems for which one is tempted to use them could be more reliably solved using templates.

```cpp
#include <iostream.h>
void copy(void *a, void *b, unsigned int size)
//copy size number of bytes from address a
//to address b
{
    for (i = 1; i <= size; ++i)
    {
//void pointers must be type cast
    *(char*)b = *(char*)a;
//characters are single bytes
    ++(char*)a;
    ++(char*)b;
    }
}
void main ()
{
 int i = 5, j = 0;
 copy(&i, &j, sizeof(int));
 cout << j;
 double x = 3.14, y = 0;
 copy(&x, &y, sizeof(double));
 cout << y;
}
```

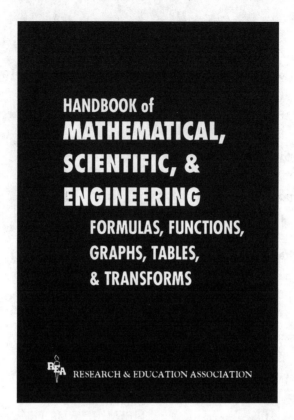

HANDBOOK of
**MATHEMATICAL,
SCIENTIFIC, &
ENGINEERING**
FORMULAS, FUNCTIONS,
GRAPHS, TABLES,
& TRANSFORMS

RESEARCH & EDUCATION ASSOCIATION

A particularly useful reference for those in math, science, engineering and other technical fields. Includes the most-often used formulas, tables, transforms, functions, and graphs which are needed as tools in solving problems. The entire field of special functions is also covered. A large amount of scientific data which is often of interest to scientists and engineers has been included.

*Available at your local bookstore or order directly from us by sending in coupon below.*

# REA's **Problem Solvers**

The "PROBLEM SOLVERS" are comprehensive supplemental text-books designed to save time in finding solutions to problems. Each "PROBLEM SOLVER" is the first of its kind ever produced in its field. It is the product of a massive effort to illustrate almost any imaginable problem in exceptional depth, detail, and clarity. Each problem is worked out in detail with a step-by-step solution, and the problems are arranged in order of complexity from elementary to advanced. Each book is fully indexed for locating problems rapidly.

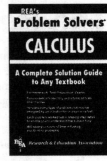

ACCOUNTING
ADVANCED CALCULUS
ALGEBRA & TRIGONOMETRY
AUTOMATIC CONTROL
   SYSTEMS/ROBOTICS
BIOLOGY
BUSINESS, ACCOUNTING, & FINANCE
CALCULUS
CHEMISTRY
COMPLEX VARIABLES
DIFFERENTIAL EQUATIONS
ECONOMICS
ELECTRICAL MACHINES
ELECTRIC CIRCUITS
ELECTROMAGNETICS
ELECTRONIC COMMUNICATIONS
ELECTRONICS
FINITE & DISCRETE MATH
FLUID MECHANICS/DYNAMICS
GENETICS
GEOMETRY
HEAT TRANSFER

LINEAR ALGEBRA
MACHINE DESIGN
MATHEMATICS for ENGINEERS
MECHANICS
NUMERICAL ANALYSIS
OPERATIONS RESEARCH
OPTICS
ORGANIC CHEMISTRY
PHYSICAL CHEMISTRY
PHYSICS
PRE-CALCULUS
PROBABILITY
PSYCHOLOGY
STATISTICS
STRENGTH OF MATERIALS &
   MECHANICS OF SOLIDS
TECHNICAL DESIGN GRAPHICS
THERMODYNAMICS
TOPOLOGY
TRANSPORT PHENOMENA
VECTOR ANALYSIS

*If you would like more information about any of these books,
complete the coupon below and return it to us or visit your local bookstore.*

---

**RESEARCH & EDUCATION ASSOCIATION**
61 Ethel Road W. • Piscataway, New Jersey 08854
Phone: (732) 819-8880     **website: www.rea.com**

**Please send me more information about your Problem Solver books**

Name _____

Address _____

City _____ State _____ Zip _____

# REA's **Test Preps**
# The Best in Test Preparation

- REA "Test Preps" are **far more** comprehensive than any other test preparation series
- Each book contains up to **eight** full-length practice tests based on the most recent exams
- **Every** type of question likely to be given on the exams is included
- Answers are accompanied by **full** and **detailed** explanations

*REA publishes over 60 Test Preparation volumes in several series. They include:*

**Advanced Placement Exams (APs)**
Biology
Calculus AB & Calculus BC
Chemistry
Computer Science
English Language & Composition
English Literature & Composition
European History
Government & Politics
Physics
Psychology
Spanish Language
Statistics
United States History

**College-Level Examination Program (CLEP)**
Analyzing and Interpreting Literature
College Algebra
Freshman College Composition
General Examinations
General Examinations Review
History of the United States I
Human Growth and Development
Introductory Sociology
Principles of Marketing
Spanish

**SAT II: Subject Tests**
Biology E/M
Chemistry
English Language Proficiency Test
French
German
Literature

**SAT II: Subject Tests (cont'd)**
Mathematics Level IC, IIC
Physics
Spanish
United States History
Writing

**Graduate Record Exams (GREs)**
Biology
Chemistry
Computer Science
General
Literature in English
Mathematics
Physics
Psychology

**ACT** - ACT Assessment

**ASVAB** - Armed Services Vocational Aptitude Battery

**CBEST** - California Basic Educational Skills Test

**CDL** - Commercial Driver License Exam

**CLAST** - College-Level Academic Skills Test

**ELM** - Entry Level Mathematics

**ExCET** - Exam for the Certification of Educators in Texas

**FE (EIT)** - Fundamentals of Engineering Exam

**FE Review** - Fundamentals of Engineering Review

**GED** - High School Equivalency Diploma Exam (U.S. & Canadian editions)

**GMAT** - Graduate Management Admission Test

**LSAT** - Law School Admission Test

**MAT** - Miller Analogies Test

**MCAT** - Medical College Admission Test

**MTEL** - Massachusetts Tests for Educator Licensure

**MSAT** - Multiple Subjects Assessment for Teachers

**NJ HSPA** - New Jersey High School Proficiency Assessment

**PLT** - Principles of Learning & Teaching Tests

**PPST** - Pre-Professional Skills Tests

**PSAT** - Preliminary Scholastic Assessment Test

**SAT I** - Reasoning Test

**SAT I** - Quick Study & Review

**TASP** - Texas Academic Skills Program

**TOEFL** - Test of English as a Foreign Language

**TOEIC** - Test of English for International Communication

---

**RESEARCH & EDUCATION ASSOCIATION**
61 Ethel Road W. • Piscataway, New Jersey 08854
Phone: (732) 819-8880    **website: www.rea.com**

### Please send me more information about your Test Prep books

Name _____

Address _____

City _____ State _____ Zip _____